MOODS IN POETRY:
A GUIDEBOOK FOR WRITERS AND READERS

by

Denise Low

Mammoth Publications, Lawrence, Kansas

© 2017 Denise Low
ISBN 978-1-939301-67-3
Library of Congress Control Number: 2017914414

Information and orders: mammothpubs@gmail.com
www.Mammoth.Publications.net

Mammoth Publications
1916 Stratford Road
Lawrence, Kansas 66044

Mammoth Publications is an independent, Indigenous-owned literary press, founded in 2003.

Author photograph by Stephan Anderson-Story
Cover photograph, land of Ken Lassman and Caryn Mirriam-Goldberg, is by the author, taken during spring burning at Wells Overlook.

Cover design assistance by Blue Heron Typesetters, 808 W. 8th Street, Silver City, NM 8806

Most of the poems in this volume are in the public domain. Other permissions are on the last page.

"I, too, dislike it: there are things that are important beyond
   all this fiddle.
  Reading it, however, with a perfect contempt for it, one
   discovers that there is in
 it after all, a place for the genuine."

                        from "Poetry" by Marianne Moore

CONTENTS

- INTRODUCTION 5
- MOODS OF POETRY: AN OVERVIEW 7
- SPELLS 13
- ROMANCE 21
- SORROW 31
- JOY 37
- AWE 45
- CELEBRATION AND ODES 51
- REFLECTION AND ODES 59
- BIOPHILIA— LOVE OF NATURE 71
- ANGER 77
- DEPRESSION 83
- HUMOR 91
- WHIMSY 99
- POEMS FOR OCCASIONS 107
- Permissions 116

INTRODUCTION

Mad as a bull? Write a rage poem. Lovelorn? Try candy, flowers, and a poem. Bored? Try a riddle poem. Or humorous verse. All shades of emotions find expression in poetry.

This collection of essays explains how poetic forms fit different moods. Some verse traditions, like sonnets, pair with romance, as basil's pungent taste enhances the sweetness of tomatoes. Infatuation fits into short, intense poems. Celebration of nature fits unhurried lines of a longer ode. Each poem is an experiment, so rules can be broken. Nonetheless, this book suggests some strategies. Prose writers may find inspiration for style.

I offer these ideas to new poets as well as veterans. When I mentioned this project to a professor, she noted how little is written about tone, voice, and mood—essentials of craft. Each chapter offers a mood, discussion, examples, best practices, and suggestions for the reader's own writing. More examples—contemporary and historic—end each chapter.

Topics are stand-alone chapters, or readers may read the entire book, front to back. Historic origins are noted, and these may be skimmed over. For in-depth understanding of the literary traditions of the English language, I include back stories.

These thoughts about moods of poetry come from my experiences with college and community writing workshops. I test-drove these ideas with an ongoing class in Kansas City. I am grateful to all the participants, especially those who attended 2016-2017: Arlin Buyert, Michael Harty, Jemshed Khan, Lindsey Martin-Bowen, Barbara Montes, Annie Newcomer, Mary Ellen Sunseri, Debbie Theiss, Diane Willie, and Erika Zeitz. Others of this workshop community that I am still in contact with include Pat Daneman, Ken Eberhart, Alan Proctor, Rhiannon Ross, and Alarie Tennille.

Thank you to my husband and co-publisher of Mammoth, Thomas Pecore Weso, who copy edits, designs, consults, listens, and cooks wonderfully well.

Denise Low, Lawrence, Kansas 2017

MOODS OF POETRY: AN OVERVIEW

Anger, joy, infatuation, grief: each casts a specific spell. Emotions may blaze or give off a slow warmth. When the poem is convincing, the emotion rekindles. Limericks set up expectations of humor. Simple rhymes are for whimsy or children's verse. Slow, measured lines are elegiac.

Some definitions: *Voice* in a poem is not mood. It is a style of expression, the imprint of the author's (or narrator's) diction. The term *narration* in literary writing is the assumed speaker, a text-based actor who presents the poem. The narrator can be another person entirely, like in the dramatic monologue of "My Last Duchess" by Robert Browning (see the end of the chapter). The literary *narrator*, also called a *persona*, can assume an autobiographical voice, but even that is a careful artifice. Narration is a tool that helps to create mood, but it is not mood itself.

Mood is closer to the literary term *tone*. Most poetry dictionaries define tone as the overall "impact" of a poem, which includes everything: content, structure, vocabulary, and poetic devices. Tone is more intellectual than mood. Irony or bafflement are examples of intellectual filters for a poem. These might develop after emotion. They are less compelling. Irony can appear in many patterns of poetry; it does not shape the form. Short and long poems, rhymed and experimental—all these can all be ironic.

Poems begin with emotion or mood—the two are nearly synonymous. Paul Muldoon writes about a poem's "preexistence," the moment before a poem comes into being. Something happens that causes a break in the ordinary flow of consciousness. That pre-poem moment has no words. It arises in the body, and forward movement through time gives it form. Its medium is words.

The Latin origin of the word "emotion" is *"e[x]movere,"* outward movement, from the embodied self. The dictionary definition of "emotion" expands on the ideas of the body and its changes: "strong feeling usually directed toward a specific object and typically accompanied by physiological and behavioral changes in the body" *(Merriam-Webster)*. The Germanic word parallel to "emotion" is "mood," derived from Old English *"mod"* (*Online Etymology Dictionary*). Its intense meanings range from courage to wrath. Mood is a stronger term than emotion, with implications of a more sustained, more powerful experience. Poets often choose the more vivid German and Anglo-Saxon terms over Latin's measured words made of prefixes and suffixes, like the word *doper* compared to *anesthesiologist.* Mood trumps emotion.

André Breton calls a poem's birth "a sublime point." This beginning of a poem can fizzle out, or it can develop into a full work of art. Lyn Hejinian calls the sequence from emotion to writing a "linkage": "one discovers the reality of *being in time*, of *taking one's chance*, of *becoming another*, all with the implicit understanding that *this is happening*" (italics are the author's). She sees the poem as unpredictable movement into a timeline. The pattern of language follows organic currents of language. Mood energizes that current.

The body's flesh and nervous systems shape poetic forms in myriad ways. One issue is how long can the brain sustain interest? Musicians are at an advantage over poets. Singers, as performers, can appeal to the body through pitches, dynamics, rhythms, and drama. Lifting a poem beyond the written page is a greater challenge. Crafting mood of a poem can help.

Aristotle, in his *Poetics,* identifies three general categories of poetry: drama, epic, and lyric. They vary greatly in (1) overall length and (2) in emphasis on story (drama and epic) or emotion (lyric). In contemporary American poetics, the most used categories are narrative and lyric, and often these overlap. The typical American poem has some elements of narrative—setting, unique point of view, beginning-to-ending arc, and often characters. Yet the predominant effect is lyric, emotion. Poetry evokes emotion more than most other literature.

Human brains dictate form through language and through limitations of capacity. People hear so many syllables, and then translate them into meaning in a brief pause. This moment of absorbing words is where a line break is helpful. Frederick Turner and Ernst Poppel did research into poetic line length and correspondence to content: "Generally a short line is used to deal with light subjects, while the long line is reserved for epic or tragic matters" (288). This makes sense, and some research supports the idea. Short lyrics are love poems or humor. Serious history or hero tales, like the *Iliad* or Shakespeare tragedies, are longer lines. Content influences form, across the globe. Turner and Poppel surveyed Chinese, Sanskrit, African, Indigenous American, and European poetry.

Mood dictates the strategies of a poem, like this poem of reflection, spiced with imagery:

First Memories by May Williams Ward
Pink-gold of grass in a vacant lot, head-high
To a three-year-old; a baby sister's hair
Bright-gold; the shade of green-cloud trees
Taking three lifts of head to see their tops—
These set the scene. My father's jiggling knee
And gaiety of song commingle sound

And rhythm. Mother's red shawl and her hair
Spill fragrance. Fragrant, too, these memories.

This poem is a quick moment of memory, with a showcase of images. The catalogue is brief, so it does not become repetitive and predictable. It reflects the fleeting quality of memory itself, which is often a few images, not a lengthy discourse This early 20th century poet captures the moment with original perspective that is still fresh.

Most often, readers encounter poetry on the printed page or illumined screen. My comments are directed to the writers more than performers of poetry. This book covers these categories of moods with suggestions for writing:

- Spells: Repetitive short phrases and refrains to effect change
- Romance: Lyrical short poems, songs, and sonnets
- Sorrow: Lyrical elegy (for lost love or lost souls), shorter poems
- Joy: Extended delight at a more conversational pace
- Awe: Short expressions of intense surprise
- Celebration: The classical ode, a longer form
- Reflection: Compositions rooted in memory and observation
- Nature Poems or Biofilia: Patterns of nature's processes
- Anger: Personal and/or rage against injustice—quick and pointed
- Depression: Less intense poems, maybe with narration
- Humor: Mixed forms with contrasts, tricksters, rhymes, irony
- Whimsy: Games, riddles, word acrobatics
- Occasional poems: poems to commemorate public events, medium length (long enough to lend gravitas). These have moods that vary.

For further thought, here is Robert Browning's masterpiece of dramatic monologue, "My Last Duchess." The narrator clearly is not Robert Browning, and the mood is, well, complicated. Readers can decide why after reading it. This story is based on historic fact. "Ferrara" is a location in northern Italy, and its duke was indeed Alfonso II, in power 1559 to 1597 (*BBC*). His wealthy first wife, Lucrezia de' Medici, died suspiciously, only two years after their marriage. The girl, a Medici, brought a large dowry to the marriage. The artists in the poem are fictitious.

My Last Duchess by Robert Browning
Ferrara
That's my last Duchess painted on the wall,
Looking as if she were alive. I call

That piece a wonder, now: Frà Pandolf's hands
Worked busily a day, and there she stands.
Will 't please you sit and look at her? I said
'Frà Pandolf' by design, for never read
Strangers like you that pictured countenance,
The depth and passion of its earnest glance,
But to myself they turned (since none puts by
The curtain I have drawn for you, but I)
And seemed as they would ask me, if they durst,
How such a glance came there; so, not the first
Are you to turn and ask thus. Sir, 't was not
Her husband's presence only, called that spot
Of joy into the Duchess' cheek: perhaps
Frà Pandolf chanced to say, 'Her mantle laps
Over my lady's wrist too much,' or 'Paint
Must never hope to reproduce the faint
Half-flush that dies along her throat:' such stuff
Was courtesy, she thought, and cause enough
For calling up that spot of joy. She had
A heart—how shall I say?—too soon made glad,
Too easily impressed; she liked whate'er
She looked on, and her looks went everywhere.
Sir, 't was all one! My favour at her breast,
The dropping of the daylight in the West,
The bough of cherries some officious fool
Broke in the orchard for her, the white mule
She rode with round the terrace—all and each
Would draw from her alike the approving speech,
Or blush, at least. She thanked men,—good! but thanked
Somehow—I know not how—as if she ranked
My gift of a nine-hundred-years-old name
With anybody's gift. Who'd stoop to blame
This sort of trifling? Even had you skill
In speech—(which I have not)—to make your will
Quite clear to such an one, and say, 'Just this
Or that in you disgusts me; here you miss,
Or there exceed the mark'—and if she let
Herself be lessoned so, nor plainly set
Her wits to yours, forsooth, and made excuse,
—E'en then would be some stooping; and I choose
Never to stoop. Oh, sir, she smiled, no doubt,
Whene'er I passed her; but who passed without
Much the same smile? This grew; I gave commands;
Then all smiles stopped together. There she stands

As if alive. Will 't please you rise? We'll meet
The company below then. I repeat,
The Count your master's known munificence
Is ample warrant that no just pretense
Of mine for dowry will be disallowed;
Though his fair daughter's self, as I avowed
At starting, is my object. Nay, we'll go
Together down, sir. Notice Neptune, though,
Taming a sea-horse, thought a rarity,
Which Claus of Innsbruck cast in bronze for me!

More Poetry Moods

From "Eyes Only" by Joseph Harrington
Picture with Aunt Mary. Picture with Uncle Pete. Summer on the patio with the Wooletts. Picture with the Woodses. She was always the one who kept the family glued, the life of the party, who got along with everyone, made sure everyone got along, even the factious Fords. She was making sure she saw everyone again. All the Dyersburg folks, at least, everyone all along again. Genealogical repair.

Spring Storm by William Carlos Williams
The sky has given over
its bitterness.
Out of the dark change
all day long
rain falls and falls
as if it would never end.
Still the snow keeps
its hold on the ground.
But water, water
from a thousand runnels!
It collects swiftly,
dappled with black
cuts a way for itself
through green ice in the gutters.
Drop after drop it falls
from the withered grass-stems
of the overhanging embankment.

Red, Red Rose by Robert Burns
O my Luve's like a red, red rose
That's newly sprung in June;
O my Luve's like the melody
That's sweetly play'd in tune.

As fair art thou, my bonnie lass,
So deep in luve am I:
And I will luve thee still, my dear,
Till a' the seas gang dry:

Till a' the seas gang dry, my dear,
And the rocks melt wi' the sun:
I will luve thee still, my dear,
While the sands o' life shall run.

And fare thee well, my only Luve
And fare thee well, a while!
And I will come again, my Luve,
Tho' it were ten thousand mile.

Snowman w/overlay by Diane Glancy
The boy made a snowman of white clay.
A showpiece, his mother said.
The blue cap he punched with holes blown back.
He said the bill curled up in the air.

The absolute zero of the circle
of the snowman's body
without the hope of anything to own
but the melting that is ahead
until finally you are left with the stick arms
to row you somewhere.

Breton, André. André Breton, *Manifestoes of Surrealism*, trans. Richard Seaver and Helen Lane. University of Michigan Press, 1969. 28.
Glancy, Diane. *It Was Then: Stories of the Elemental.* Mammoth, 2012.
Harrington, Joseph. From "Eyes Only." *Things Come On: [An Amneoir]*. Wesleyan University Press, 2011. 28.
Hejinian, Lyn. *The Language of Inquiry.* The University of California Press, 2000. 3.
Muldoon, Paul. *End of the Poem.* Farrar & Strauss, 2006; "Interview." *Paris Review* 87.
Turner, Frederick and Ernst Poppel, "The Neural Lyre: Poetic Meter, the Brain, and Time" (*Poetry*, Aug. 1983: 277-309).
Ward, May Williams. *Prairie Rhythms,* ed. Lana Wirt Myers. Mammoth, 2010.

SPELLS

The first poems are spells, words designed to make changes in reality. Prayers can be in this category: "Give us this day our daily bread." Children's chants, like "Rain, rain, go away," can be magical thinking, based on the assumption that words influence outcomes. Poker players have a repertoire of sayings, like "Cut 'em thin, bound to win" and "Cut 'em thick, beat 'em quick." Some phrases make legal contracts: "I now pronounce you husband and wife." "I dare you" is another command that is a real-time action. These examples are "performative" in linguistic lingo: "Relating to or denoting an utterance by means of which the speaker performs a particular act (e.g. *I bet, I apologize, I promise*)" (Oxford Dictionary). The word is binding. Oaths are performative, as are spells.

Words have not only performative results, but also physical impact as they create reactions from sensory imagery (all five senses) and abstractions. Audiences in horror movies have physiological reactions of fear. Good writing causes such responses. My first poetry mentor said to be careful what I wrote about, because it could become a reality. He was a very logical guy, and I was surprised that this was his first advice. He impressed me. Through the years, I have come to believe there is a truth here. Our thoughts about ourselves, our personal narratives, are very powerful magnets. We find like-minded friends. We shape experiences based on our inner scripts.

Words impact our surroundings. Masaru Emoto, a Japanese scientist published *Messages from Water*, basis of the movie *What the Bleep Do We Know?* His book contains photographs of ice crystals and accompanying experiments. Water samples freezing into ice crystals develop differently based on exposure to music. Those exposed to heavy-metal rock and roll show disorder in form; those exposed to harmonious music ("Amazing Grace") create symmetrical structures. This may or may not hold up to further experimental research, but music therapy is a related field of inquiry that supports the concept.

I remember being in a deep depression once, and I imagined quartz crystals for a few minutes. It did not solve problems, but this image calmed me immediately. Reflecting pools soothe almost everyone. Poets have power to effect changes in the people around them, and perhaps even water itself.

The Trance of Spell

Here is the end of a *Diné* (Navajo) walking prayer-song. The word *hozho* implies balance, harmony with the natural world, and beauty. The English word is often just "beauty."

By This Song I Walk, by Andrew Natonabah
By this song I walk.
Long Life,
By it I am Beautiful.
By this song I walk.
By this song I walk.
By this song I walk.
By this song I walk.
From Pollen I am looked upon.
By this song I walk.
Flowers teach me.
By this song I walk.
Corn Beetle sounds behind me.
By this song I walk.
Bluebird sounds before me.
By this song I walk. ...

This is a contemporary example of age-old spells used to create a harmonious effect.

Xánath Caraza's poem "Yanga" uses spell-like repetition in her homage to a Mexican hero from Vera Cruz, Louis Reyes Rivera. Repetitions evoke his memory and renew his power.

Yanga by Xánath Caraza
Yanga, Yanga, Yanga
Yanga, Yanga, Yanga
Today, your spirit I invoke
Here, in this place

This, this is my poem for Yanga
Mandinga, malanga, bamba
Rumba, mambo, samba.
Words having arrived from Africa

This, this is my answer for Yanga
Candomble, mocambo, mambo
Candomble, mocambo, mambo
Free man of Veracruz
In 1570
You arrived at the Port of Veracruz
In chains as many
You escaped slavery

Palenque, rumba, samba
Yanga, Yanga, Yanga
Unconquerable spirit
Noble man from Africa

In 1609
You fought for freedom
At your doors, they arrived and
They couldn't come in

Mandinga, malanga, bamba
Palenque, rumba, samba
Palenque, rumba, samba
Pride, rhythm and freedom

By 1630
San Lorenzo de los negros
Was established
Today, the town of Yanga

Candomble, mocambo, mambo
Yanga, Yanga, Yanga
Today, your spirit I invoke
Here, in this place

Yanga, Yanga, Yanga
Palenque, rumba, samba
Mandinga, malanga, bamba
Candomble, mocambo, mambo

Condomble, mocambo, mambo
Mandinga, malanga, bamba
Palenque, rumba, samba
Yanga, Yanga, Yanga

When Caraza presents this poem, the walls shake. Audio recordings of it are available on the website *Phonodia*.

Spells of Pronouncement

Langston Hughes uses a Walt Whitman-like rhetoric to make pronouncements about America in his poem "Let America Be America Again" —and in the process, he articulates a political and moral stance. His writings laid groundwork for the Civil Rights Movement. He inspires, and he also encourages listeners to enact the ideals of the United States: "O, let my land be a land where Liberty / Is crowned with no false patriotic wreath, / But opportunity is real, and life is free."

This epithalamion (marriage) poem centers on the implied vow, "I do," a performative verb. The list extends the oath of commitment:

> **I Marry Your by Denise Low**
> I marry your late lamplight insomnia
> I marry your pierced ear lobe with no earring, half closed
> I marry your political views
> I marry your stepfather who disappeared
> I marry your warm hand's fleshy comfort
> I marry your sweet silky skin laid against mine
> I marry your stereo system thumping acid rock
> I marry socks, underwear, and shirts you cannot sort
> I marry your slow-cooked pork with sauerkraut
> I marry your tears when Uncle Buddy died
> I marry your voice, its music of short vowels
> I marry the twenty-odd years you have stacked your
>   socks, underwear and shirts in the closet next to mine.

This is a catalogue poem I wrote as illustration. It shows the active part of a transitive verb.

Techniques for Writing Spell Poems

- Rhythm is an essential ingredient to a spell.
- Parallel construction of sentences, locating the repeating pattern at the front end of a line rather than the end, is an effective way to build a spell.
- Repetition can build intensity. Third time is a charm, as the fairy tales say, or four times in many Indigenous American traditions (or seven or twelve).
- Vary the repetitious pattern so that syntax as well as content do not become monotonous. Caraza's poem is an example of a good balance between repetition and variation.
- Use of a stanzaic refrain can stress the oath or spell, also.
- Balance of specific details with abstract ideas (freedom, marriage) helps to keep a rhythm of content and well as form.

Suggestions for Your Writing

- Write a poem that makes a real pronouncement, dare, vow, prayer, or other performative gesture in words.
- Write a spell for a natural occurrence, like to bring snow.

⊕ Write a set of wishes for the year to come. Begin each wish with the same phrase. Some people do this each new moon or each birthday.

More Spell Poems:

Seder Checklist by Danny Caine
Holiday candles
One bottle Wine
    Eh, bring a good one
    Eh, bring a liter of Manischevitz too
Seder Plate
Cup for Elijah
    Don't forget the Rite Lite Ten Plagues Toy Kit
Three matzot, covered
A plate of pickles, hidden
    for these cousins, pickles are like money
Salt water for dipping
Cup, basin, towel for washing
    Eh, what's the difference if I use the sink
At least one shiksa girlfriend
Haggadah for each person
    even the girlfriend
Wine cup for each person
    except the two youngest cousins
    and the girlfriend

Optional:
Matzoh of Hope
    Harold? What on earth is a Matzoh of Hope?
Afikomen bag
Empty plate to remember the homeless
Empty plate to remember those in the diaspora of death
Empty plate to remember those in the diaspora of *divorce*
Empty plates to remember the 4 sons who moved away
    Where are we gonna put all these empty plates?

The Bells by Edgar Allan Poe

I.
Hear the sledges with the bells —
Silver bells!
What a world of merriment their melody foretells!
How they tinkle, tinkle, tinkle,
In the icy air of night!
While the stars that oversprinkle
All the heavens, seem to twinkle
With a crystalline delight;
Keeping time, time, time,
In a sort of Runic rhyme,
To the tintinnabulation that so musically wells
From the bells, bells, bells, bells,
Bells, bells, bells —
From the jingling and the tinkling of the bells.

II.
Hear the mellow wedding-bells
Golden bells!
What a world of happiness their harmony foretells!
Through the balmy air of night
How they ring out their delight! —
From the molten-golden notes,
And all in tune,
What a liquid ditty floats
To the turtle-dove that listens, while she gloats
On the moon!
Oh, from out the sounding cells,
What a gush of euphony voluminously wells!
How it swells!
How it dwells
On the Future! — how it tells
Of the rapture that impels
To the swinging and the ringing
Of the bells, bells, bells —
Of the bells, bells, bells, bells,
Bells, bells, bells —
To the rhyming and the chiming of the bells!

III.
Hear the loud alarm bells —
Brazen bells!
What a tale of terror, now, their turbulency tells!
In the startled ear of night
How they scream out their affright!
Too much horrified to speak,
They can only shriek, shriek,
Out of tune,
In a clamorous appealing to the mercy of the fire,
In a mad expostulation with the deaf and frantic fire,
Leaping higher, higher, higher,
With a desperate desire,
And a resolute endeavor
Now — now to sit, or never,
By the side of the pale-faced moon.
Oh, the bells, bells, bells!
What a tale their terror tells
Of Despair!
How they clang, and clash, and roar!
What a horror they outpour
On the bosom of the palpitating air!
Yet the ear, it fully knows,
By the twanging
And the clanging,
How the danger ebbs and flows;
Yet [[Yes]], the ear distinctly tells,
In the jangling
And the wrangling,
How the danger sinks and swells,
By the sinking or the swelling in the anger of the bells —
Of the bells —
Of the bells, bells, bells, bells,
Bells, bells, bells —
In the clamour and the clangour of the bells!

IV.
Hear the tolling of the bells —
Iron bells!
What a world of solemn thought their monody compels!
In the silence of the night,
How we shiver with affright
At the melancholy menace of their tone!
For every sound that floats

From the rust within their throats
Is a groan.
And the people — ah, the people —
They that dwell up in the steeple,
All alone,
And who, tolling, tolling, tolling,
In that muffled monotone,
Feel a glory in so rolling
On the human heart a stone —
They are neither man nor woman —
They are neither brute nor human —
They are Ghouls: —
And their king it is who tolls: —
And he rolls, rolls, rolls, rolls,
Rolls
A pæan from the bells!
And his merry bosom swells
With the pæan of the bells!
And he dances, and he yells;
Keeping time, time, time,
In a sort of Runic rhyme,
To the pæan of the bells —
Of the bells: —
Keeping time, time, time,
In a sort of Runic rhyme,
To the throbbing of the bells —
Of the bells, bells, bells —
To the sobbing of the bells: —
Keeping time, time, time,
As he knells, knells, knells,
In a happy Runic rhyme,
To the rolling of the bells —
Of the bells, bells, bells: —
To the tolling of the bells —
Of the bells, bells, bells, bells,
Bells, bells, bells —
To the moaning and the groaning of the bells.

Caine, Danny. *Uncle Harold's Maxwell House Haggadah*. Etchings Press, 2017. 3.
Caraza, Xanath. "Yanga." *Conjuro*. Mammoth Publications, 2012. 35. Audio file: *Phonodia*. Accessed 28 Aug. 2017.
Emoto, Masaru. *The Hidden Messages in Water*. Simon & Schuster, 2011.
Natonabah, Andrew. "By This Song I Walk." *Native Literature from the Southwest*. 1978. Accessed 28 Aug. 2017.

ROMANCE

Infatuation, passion, crush, craze—these words try to communicate the temporary-insanity stage of love. Greeks recognized fraternal and religious love, separate from eroticism. Only Eros was a designated love god.

Aristotle's category of "lyric" poetry is verse sung or recited with a lyre. Lyrical short poems, songs, and sonnets are ideally suited to address the quick passion of romantic love. Long-term marriage love is another genre, with celebration of domestic as well as romantic moments—the shared dog or plums in the refrigerator. These are less urgent.

The infatuation poem remains one of the most exciting in the English language. It is sexually charged, focused, and dramatically addressed to the beloved. It is an aspect of courtship, so it borrows from spells. The lyrics of many popular American songs, like "I Want to Hold Your Hand" (the Beatles) and "Satisfaction" (Rolling Stones), are perfect Eros-oriented rhymes. They are not complicated. The mood of passion calls for quick formats.

Direct Address

Sappho, who lived around 600 B.C. E., is the earliest lyric poet in the Western European literary tradition, which informs the English language. Sappho, from the island of Lesbos, wrote many love poems. All have immediacy, as though the beloved were in the room with her. She uses a direct, first-person "I" to address to the loved one. This resembles the religious address to the gods or the Muse, the "Oh" of a prayer, "Oh Lord." The ritual syllable "oh" opens a plea. The love poem is secular, but it resonates with religious diction.

Here the narrator is almost a voice-over in the opening of a film:

Fragment 31 by Sappho
Look at him, just like a god,
that man sitting across from you,
whoever he is, listening to your
  close, sweet voice,

your irresistible laughter and O yes,
it sets my heart racing—
one glance at you and I can't
  get any words out,

my voice cracks, a thin flame
runs under my skin,

my eyes see nothing,
my ears ring,

a cold sweat pours down my body,
I tremble all over, turn
paler than grass, and it seems that I'm
just a shade from dead.

But I must bear it, since a poor. . .. (trans. Stanley Lombardo)

The rest of the poem is lost, but this love poem shows physical reactions to mood. The lover narrates a dramatic situation perfect for extreme metaphors, like "a thin flame runs under my skin." This Sapphic convention set a pattern for the centuries.

Sonnets

The sonnet form adapts to romantic uses, perhaps because it meets the needs of both short-term and long-term memory. It reflects a need for ordered passion, the human paradox. Too much order leads to boredom.

The term sonnet comes from the Italian word for song, *sonetto*. The derivation from a song form is apparent in its brevity and pattern: fourteen lines written in rhymed iambic pentameter (five accents a line with stress on each second syllable). There are several different rhyme schemes, and the easiest in English is the Shakespearean sonnet: ababcdcd, efef, gg. Notice the first eight lines have two sets of rhymes (Italian has only variations on two rhymes). The first eight lines present a problem, the next four a possible resolution, and the final couplet is a slantways conclusion.

The sonnet often refers to romance as an eternal, uplifting, and spiritual experience. Italian (Petrarchan), Spenserian, and Shakespearean sonnets are well-known forms in European poetics. Contemporary American poets often use a looser version that may not have the exact structure of the Renaissance sonnet, but it does continue the spirit.

Shakespeare writes some of the most enduring love poems in the sonnet form. He embeds romance in nature itself with this homage to springtime. He lifts mortal love into an eternal time. This is not ordinary love, but rather a celebration of the loved one's beauty in mythic terms. This is one of the most enduring of Shakespeare's works, with extended the extended metaphor announced in the opening and sustained throughout the poem:

Sonnet 18 by William Shakespeare
Shall I compare thee to a summer's day?
Thou art more lovely and more temperate:
Rough winds do shake the darling buds of May,
And summer's lease hath all too short a date;
Sometime too hot the eye of heaven shines,
And often is his gold complexion dimm'd;
And every fair from fair sometime declines,

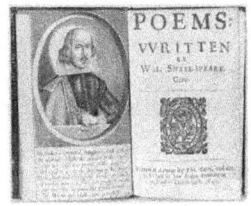

By chance or nature's changing course untrimm'd;
But thy eternal summer shall not fade,
Nor lose possession of that fair thou ow'st;
Nor shall death brag thou wander'st in his shade,
When in eternal lines to time thou grow'st:
  So long as men can breathe or eyes can see,
  So long lives this, and this gives life to thee.

A contrast is a lesser known Shakespearean sonnet that is darker than most, but the passion is palpable:

Sonnet 147 by William Shakespeare
My love is as a fever, longing still
For that which longer nurseth the disease,
Feeding on that which doth preserve the ill,
Th' uncertain sickly appetite to please.
My reason, the physician to my love,
Angry that his prescriptions are not kept,
Hath left me, and I desperate now approve
Desire is death, which physic did except.

Past cure I am, now reason is past care,
And frantic-mad with evermore unrest;
My thoughts and my discourse as madmen's are,
At random from the truth vainly expressed:
  For I have sworn thee fair, and thought thee bright,
  Who art as black as hell, as dark as night.

The narrator is "frantic-mad" and he concludes the disappointing lover is "black as hell." The pace of the lines, the assertive diction, the comparison to physical disease—all these are the angry words of a spurned lover.
   What I call "slant" sonnets, then, are contemporary love poems that follow the spirit of the sonnet pattern. Like slant rhyme, they are less direct. Slant sonnets may describe traditional topics of love—courtship, celebration

of the beloved, passion, requited and/or unrequited longing—in shortish poems that focus bursts of emotion. The technique is heightened language. A slant sonnet may not rhyme or scan a regular rhythm, but nonetheless, the poem is a sonnet, with these shared characteristics:

- Relatively short, ten to twenty lines line, to sustain lyric intensity
- Relatively similar line lengths and pattern
- Consistent diction with tightly related imagery
- Presentation of a "problem" of universal theme, like unrequited love or the passing of time, in the opening section
- Turn or *volta* at the halfway mark or just after
- A digression into a solution or secondary set of images or narration
- An unexpected twist in the last line or two

Here is an example of a contemporary "slant sonnet" from Greg Field's book *Black Heart*:

The Story I Tell You by Greg Field
I want to read something to you, because
I love you. Through the window I see
the roofs and cooling units and the useless
chimneys clogged with dead birds.
But I want to read something to you, because
I love you. So I read you the window's story.

I read you the story I see across the glass
and tar paper roofs. The story of the old man
opening the pigeon coop, reaching in slowly
and bringing out a delicate bird
with strong markings, cradled like a heart
just removed from a young, impetuous donor,
and releasing it into the ever expanding sky.

This is thirteen lines, not fourteen. Some lines begin with accented words, and some do not. Some ends of lines repeat words or sounds, but not in a pattern. But the turn in the second stanza, second line, "The story of the old man" is a definite pivot point or *volta*. The ending of the poem is the astonishing image of a bird being compared to the lover's beating heart. The "ever expanding sky" is the moment where the poem lifts into the realm of the heavens. Scansion is secondary to the feel of the poem.

Poignant Love: Asian Poems

Each November my grandmother reread her translations of Chinese and Japanese poetry, especially T'Ang dynasty poets. She loved to weep as her birthday recurred (she lived to 94) and as leaves blew in the wind. I loved that she loved this tradition of poems. They fit her old age well.

Asian languages are so different from English, that translations are approximations that fit into neither literary tradition exactly. The calligraphy context is lost. Tonal puns are lost. Allusions to symbols of season, festivals, and places are less clear. Yet Asian forms of haiku, tanka, and others continue to attract English-language poets. Brevity, syllable count, and seasonal references remain, as well as koan-like moments at the end. This poem by Ch'en Shu Pao (Hou Chu, 553-604, Ch'en Dynasty) is typical of the love poems from my grandmother's books:

Longing by Ch'en Shu Pao
Since you have gone,
My love,
The grass grows green and long
Upon the unused terrace steps.
For love of you
I am like yonder lamp,
Which seems to weep
And shed hot tears of longing
As it burns
Through the long and dreary watches
Of the night.

This defines romantic pining for the loved one, with use of images—"unused terrace steps," "hot tears." Descriptions parallel the narrator's mood. Often translators of Asian poetry abandon rhyme, as in this 1938 translation. Images are more important and reinforce the Imagist poets like H.D. and Ezra Pound. This differs from the European tradition, yet basics remain. This Chinese poem is brief, filled with emotion, and unforgettable—like all good love poems.

Here is a love poem filled with regret and ephemera, from William Sheldon:

Boards by William Sheldon
The way you can sand a joint
until the crack almost
disappears, the grain of two boards

seeming to meet in a sane pattern.
So too should be all my endeavors—
playing catch with my children,

weeding the garden, making love
with my wife, writing this poem.

But there is a restlessness in boards,
born of long stillness in the trunk,
while the slim, ethereal top branches
shimmered in the nomad breeze,
while the leaves yearly deserted,
and the roots sought new pools.
So when they can,
boards will warp
giving themselves
up to the will of water, to movement
that is no fault of their own.

The "boards" take over the poem, as they represent the impersonal and inevitable process of aging. The mood is poignant, with love as part of the poet's regret about the passage of time. The Asian influence here is in the theme of transience and in the vivid images. This hybrid poem also shows echoes of the British tradition, in its lines and ode-like reflection. The yielding of human foibles to larger natural forces is typical of Sheldon's work. The self-deprecating grasslands attitude, that humility, is present in his voice. The ending reaches beyond personal romance.

More Than Stars in the Skies

More types of love poems exist—they are as infinite as the human imagination, and our species has no problem with continuing the generations. The most passionate poems are lightning strikes, not slow rise of floodwaters. Drama is essential, as well as specific details.

Some helpful strategies:
- ⊕ Generalities kill love poem. Personalize your writing.
- ⊕ Balance personal and universal. The private love language of a couple may not translate to a public medium effectively.
- ⊕ Sentimentality—unearned emotion—is the foe of effective love poems.
- ⊕ Clichés abound, since love poems are so old. Read widely to know what has been done already.

Suggestions for Your Writing
- Write a love poem based on one color for imagery.
- Write a love poem in first-person "I," and then rewrite it in second-person "you," and third-person "he/she." Review each for impact. Consider other genders.
- Remember your first romance. Write a love poem from your adult point of view.
- Choose a love poem, European or Asian, as a model. Look at its architecture and imitate it.
- Fall in love and imitate any of the love poems in this section.

More Love Poems

We Two, How Long We Were Fool'd by Walt Whitman

We two, how long we were fool'd,
Now transmuted, we swiftly escape as Nature escapes,
We are Nature, long have we been absent, but now we return,
We become plants, trunks, foliage, roots, bark,
We are bedded in the ground, we are rocks,
We are oaks, we grow in the openings side by side,
We browse, we are two among the wild herds spontaneous as any,
We are two fishes swimming in the sea together,
We are what locust blossoms are, we drop scent around lanes mornings and evenings,
We are also the coarse smut of beasts, vegetables, minerals,
We are two predatory hawks, we soar above and look down,
We are two resplendent suns, we it is who balance ourselves orbic and stellar, we are as two comets,
We prowl fang'd and four-footed in the woods, we spring on prey,
We are two clouds forenoons and afternoons driving overhead,
We are seas mingling, we are two of those cheerful waves rolling over each other and interwetting each other,
We are what the atmosphere is, transparent, receptive, pervious, impervious,
We are snow, rain, cold, darkness, we are each product and influence of the globe,
We have circled and circled till we have arrived home again, we two,
We have voided all but freedom and all but our own joy.

A Love Song by William Carlos Williams
What have I to say to you
When we shall meet?
Yet—
I lie here thinking of you.

The stain of love
Is upon the world.
Yellow, yellow, yellow,
It eats into the leaves,
Smears with saffron
The horned branches that lean
Heavily
Against a smooth purple sky.

There is no light—
Only a honey-thick stain
That drips from leaf to leaf
And limb to limb
Spoiling the colours
Of the whole world.

I am alone.
The weight of love
Has buoyed me up
Till my head
Knocks against the sky.

See me!
My hair is dripping with nectar—
Starlings carry it
On their black wings.
See, at last
My arms and my hands
Are lying idle.

How can I tell
If I shall ever love you again
As I do now?

from Defining Things by Mercedes Lucero

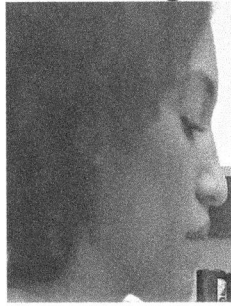

Origin:
mid-June; Our bodies were like magnets drawn to each other, to the way we moved, to the way our chests rose and fell, to the way our eyes met for brief moments before they lost each other, to the way our bodies looked when we were awake, wilting away in the naked summer sun, and to the way our bodies looked when we slept softly, as if we were dead.

Francesca by Ezra Pound

You came in out of the night
And there were flowers in your hands,
Now you will come out of a confusion of people,
Out of a turmoil of speech about you.
I who have seen you amid the primal things
Was angry when they spoke your name
In ordinary places.
I would that the cool waves might flow over my mind,
And that the world should dry as a dead leaf,
Or as a dandelion seed-pod and be swept away,
So that I might find you again,
Alone.

Sonnet IV by Edna St. Vincent Millay

I shall forget you presently, my dear,
So make the most of this, your little day,
Your little month, your little half a year
Ere I forget, or die, or move away,
And we are done forever; by and by
I shall forget you, as I said, but now,
If you entreat me with your loveliest lie
I will protest you with my favorite vow.
I would indeed that love were longer-lived,
And vows were not so brittle as they are,
But so it is, and nature has contrived
To struggle on without a break thus far,—
Whether or not we find what we are seeking
Is idle, biologically speaking.

This Much and More by Djuna Barnes
If my lover were a comet
    Hung in air,
I would braid my leaping body
    In his hair.
Yea, if they buried him ten leagues
    Beneath the loam,
My fingers they would learn to dig
    And I'd plunge home!

Dear L – by Judith Roitman
Dear L –
    The bag broke but I didn't know what was going on. It wasn't even our mattress. I believed everything you said: moon, chicken soup, ferry, matches. I threw books at the wall, at the floor, anywhere but her head, leaping onto glass—who could see it?—the quick trip to the infirmary. And the Shruti box—how wee we supposed to know what it was, or that it would be wielded so suddenly? I wonder what's reversed, nobody's body is ever the same, but it was so easy to trace you down, even my grandfather was able to do it. And now it's 4 of 42, 1555 of 1677. This is how it fills in, no blanks left and no mystery either.

Field, Greg. "The Story I Tell You." *Black Heart*. Mammoth, 2014. 31.
Ch'en, Shu Pao. "Longing." Trans. Henry H. Hart. *A Garden of Peonies*. Stanford University Press, 1938.
Lucero, Mercedes. "Defining Things." *In the Garden of Broken Things*. Flutter Press, 2016. 7.
Roitman, Judith. "Dear L—." *Slackline*. Hank's Original Loose Gravel Press, 2012. 15.
Sappho, translated by Stanley Lombardo. "Fragment 31." *Complete Poems and Fragments*. Hackett, 2017. 19.
Sheldon, William. "Boards." *Rain Comes Riding*. Mammoth, 2013. 50.
Williams, William Carlos. "Love Poem." *Poems,* 2016. *Academy of American Poets*.

SORROW

Sorrow has its own form in the poetic tradition—elegy. The short, lyrical elegy fits the occasion of grief most directly. Its brevity can suggest the pang of tragedy. Longer ode-like reflections fit sorrow. The response to death is the most common form of elegy, although other kinds of elegies are possible. The American English elegy evolves out of a Roman elegiac couplet form, but the two-lined stanza pattern is seldom used now. Elegies are related to epitaphs, odes, and eulogies. Here are some differences: Epitaphs are brief; odes celebrate rather than mourn; and eulogies are prose. There is no specific pattern for the elegy, although it is a public mode of poetry. A set pattern for public expression of grief might evolve. For now, readers recognize an elegy from title, formal diction, and an internal move from grief to consolation.

Historic Origins of Elegies

Elegy comes from the Greek work *elegus*, which means a song of lament, accompanied by an *aulos* (flute). The word is from Greek (possibly Ionian) funerary poems that begin: "ε, λεγε ε, λεγε - Woe, cry woe, cry!" The tradition began as a public poem, often about a public personage. The range of subjects could include love, war, and death:

It was...the vehicle for exhortation and for reflection on a variety of themes—warfare, politics, ethics, man's life in general. Its form helped the poet to marshal his ideas into brief, striking phrases, often made more memorable by the balance and even the internal rhyme of the pentameter. (Campbell)

Poetry in the Greek language had set patterns that signaled content, as a limerick in English sets up expectations with its opening line. The Greek elegy form signaled a general "woe is me" message, not strictly funerary.

Ovid, Catullus, and Propertius are well-known Roman elegists. They developed the elegiac couplet, which is dactyl (the metric count is: stress, unstressed, unstressed), the preferred form for serious works like the *Aeneid*. The Roman-style elegiac couplet is a line of six stresses (hexameter) followed by a line of five stresses (pentameter). The idea of lament was consistent, but the subject matter was variable, including even an erotic variation. Ovid wrote about the uneven lines as rising and falling: "*Sex mihi surgat opus numeris, in quinque residat*- Let my work rise in six steps, fall back in five." (*Amores* I.1.27). The accents were important. Samuel Coleridge describes elegies as:

> In the hexameter rises the fountain's silvery column,
> In the pentameter aye falling in melody back. (*Specimens*)

Throughout the Medieval period, Christians used the elegy form for hymns, with death transformed into Christian triumph. The couplet and quatrain also adapted to use as epitaphs on tombstones or funerary tablets (see the epitaph example by King James below). The idea of epitaph and elegiac meter began to telescope into one form, yet as late as the 19th century, Coleridge wrote of the elegy as a personal lyric:

> Elegy is a form of poetry natural to the reflective mind. It may treat of any subject, but it must treat of no subject for itself; but always and exclusively with reference to the poet. As he will feel regret for the past or desire for the future, so sorrow and love became the principal themes of the elegy. Elegy presents everything as lost and gone or absent and future. (*Specimens*)

The Elegiac Arc: Sorrow to Triumph

The classical elegy begins with a very public invocation of the muse and then further context of traditional Graeco-Roman mythology, as in this example by James VI of Scotland/James I of England, about the courier Philip Sidney. The individual voice expresses personal loss in a dialectic with public honor for a fallen citizen:

> **An Epitaph on Sir Philip Sidney, by King James I/VI**
> Thou mighty Mars, the god of soldiers brave,
> And thou, Minerva, that does in wit excel,
> And thou, Apollo, that does knowledge have
> Of every art that from Parnassus fell,
> With all the Sisters that thereon do dwell
> Lament for him who duly served you all,
> Whom in you wisely all your arts did mell,
> Bewail, I say, his unexpected fall.
> I need not in remembrance for to call
> His youth, his race, the hope had of him aye
> Since that in him doth cruel death appall
> Both manhood, wit, and learning every way
>   Now in the bed of honor doth he rest
>   And evermore of him shall live the best.

"Mell" means mix and "aye" means every. In this 1586 poem, King James invokes Mars, Minerva, Apollo, and then the Muses (the "Sisters"). The range of Roman gods indicates his many ranges of talents, from military to the arts. This is praise for the departed man, indirectly, until the sixth through eighth lines, which identify the loss and the man's relationship to the divine beings: "Lament" and "Bewail, I say," are imperative commands as well as public announcement of the death.

In the poem's arc come invocation, announcement, and then memories, abbreviated here. Other poets might spend more time recounting virtues of the deceased. But brevity captures grief more immediately. Next is acknowledgement of the greater force of death. Some poets take this stage and expound on the problem of human mortality. Here is an opportunity for poetic forays. Themes of destiny, justice and fate may be woven into the individual loss. Finally comes the apotheosis, or transformation of the deceased into a being with greater spiritual qualities—honor, eternal "rest," and the continuing "best" of the man. This is, somewhat, a comfort.

I wonder about the 17th century sensibility, when different denominations of Christians persecuted each other violently, yet invocation of the pagan Classical world was allowed. James I/VI was at the nexus of bloodshed between Catholics and Protestants. Somehow, literature created a neutral space where former gods are powerful beings. This ritual invocation of the Muses persisted for centuries.

Greek and Roman mythology continues to populate various arts genres and English language poetry today. Louise Gluck works with the Graeco-Roman literary tradition in notable ways, as does Anne Carson.

In American poetry, early examples of elegies are Walt Whitman's "O Captain, My Captain," about the death of Abraham Lincoln, and Anne Bradstreet's "epitaphs," among many others. Bradstreet lived from 1612 to 1672, and her Puritan religion echoes in her poems. Death of a child is heartbreaking, and multiple losses of children— or "flours" [flowers]—even more so. The triumph of belief in the face of grief is the focus of this elegy:

On My Dear Grand-Child Simon Bradstreet, Who Dyed On 16.Novemb. 1669. Being But a Moneth, and One D[ay]
by Anne Bradstreet
No sooner come, but gone, and fal'n asleep,
Acquaintance short, yet parting caus'd us weep,
Three flours, two scarcely blown, the last i' th' bud,
Cropt by th'Almighties hand; yet is he good,
With dreadful awe before him let's be mute,
Such was his will, but why, let's not dispute,

With humble hearts and mouths put in the dust,
Let's say he's merciful as well as just.
He will return, and make up all our losses,
And smile again, after our bitter crosses.
Go pretty babe, go rest with Sisters twain
Among the blest in endless joyes remain.

Contemporary Variables of Elegies

The American elegist may leave out the muses and other invocations, or not. The apotheosis may occur, or not. Another way to consider the architecture of an elegy is the Kubler-Ross cycle of grief, which can appear as: denial (or shock), anger, bargaining, depression, and acceptance. This can be seen simplified into three stages: "First, there is a lament, where the speaker expresses grief and sorrow, then praise and admiration of the idealized dead, and finally consolation and solace" (Academy of American Poets).

Grieving for loss can be for a person, or it can by for a place. The Yupik scholar and author Oscar Kawagley, of Northern Alaska, who tells about the grieving process for communities inundated by rising sea levels—Heartbeat, Kivaline, Kiana. These villages had to plan ways to move inland. First, though, they grieved as a group and individually for the loss of their homes.

DaMaris Hill observes the city of Wichita as "wet with regret," "divorced," and otherwise isolated. It is an elegy for a place:

> **night watch and what of wichita by DaMaris Hill**
> **(37.6889° N, 97.3361° W)**
> twilight and night are tufting, buttoning into rose dawn, making velvet ribbons from black's memories. hell's flames crescendo in the sky. i listen expecting voices. i am desperate to know why this place is wet with regret. divorced and no longer remembers how to collect and return the waters, a place that pouts and puckers before rain pours.

Hill's prose poem shows how an elegy can be unmoored from even line breaks. Emphasis is on image and surprising juxtapositions of words. These create the extreme emotion of the poem.

Considerations When Writing an Elegy:
- ⊕ If you don't use traditional elegiac couplets, create regular stanzas.
- ⊕ Architecture of the loss poem moves from grief to consolation.
- ⊕ Contrast the tension between private grief and cultural ideas about death and rituals.

- Public figures can represent culture and history—Prince, John F. Kennedy, Emily Dickinson, Philip Sidney, Keats.
- Occasions other than death might merit an elegy, such as loss of a building or natural object. I grieved the loss of the yard's maple.

Suggestions for Writing
- Write an elegy to a childhood memory or childhood friend.
- Write an elegy for yourself. What discoveries occur?
- Choose a favo4rite public figure who died in the last year. Write an elegy for this person, including what he/she meant to you.
- Expand a private elegy through public context—does a person represent a passing of something historic?
- Remember a childhood place you loved and write an elegy for it.

More Poems of Sorrow

Elegy by D.H. Lawrence
The sun immense and rosy
Must have sunk and become extinct
The night you closed your eyes for ever against me.

Grey days, and wan, dree dawnings
Since then, with fritter of flowers –
Day wearies me with its ostentation and fawnings.

Still, you left me the nights,
The great dark glittery window,
The bubble hemming this empty existence with lights.

Still in the vast hollow
Like a breath in a bubble spinning
Brushing the stars, goes my soul, that skims the bounds like a
    [swallow?

I can look through
The film of the bubble night, to where you are.
Through the film I can almost touch you.

Telling Time by Jo McDougall
My son and I walk away
from his sister's day-old grave.
Our backs to the sun,
the forward pitch of our shadows
tells us the time.
By sweetest accident
he inclines
his shadow,
touching mine.

Face by James Weldon Johnson
The glory of the day was in her face,
The beauty of the night was in her eyes.
And over all her loveliness, the grace
Of Morning blushing in the early skies.
And in her voice, the calling of the dove;
Like music of a sweet, melodious part.
And in her smile, the breaking light of love;
And all the gentle virtues in her heart.

And now the glorious day, the beauteous night,
The birds that signal to their mates at dawn,
To my dull ears, to my tear-blinded sight
Are one with all the dead, since she is gone.

Campbell, D.A. "Elegy." *Greek Lyric Poetry*. 1967. London.
Coleridge, Samuel. *Specimens of the Table Talk of the Late Samuel Taylor Coleridge*, II. John Murray, 1835: 268.
Hill, DaMaris. *Visible Textures*. Mammoth, 2015. 20.
Kawagley, Angayuqaq Oscar. "Talk." *Impact of Climate Change on Indigenous Peoples June 19-22, 2006 Symposium*. CReSIS.
McDougall, Jo. "Telling Time." *In the Home of the Famous Dead: Collected Poems*. University of Arkansas Press, 2015.
Rilke, Rainer Maria. *Poems,* 1918, translated by Jessie Lemont. Web.

JOY

The counterpart to grief is joy. In language, it can be a shout or "whee!" or Walt Whitman's "yawp": "I sound my barbaric yawp over the rooftops of the world." This mood is not the extended, public celebration of an ode. A joyous poem is brief, focused, and emotional.

Sublime human experiences that evoke bursts of pleasure may include: birth of a child, discovery of the perfect truffle, inspiration on a mountain, recognition of an old friend. These can be topics of poetry, and the short lyric is a perfect vehicle. Otherwise, no single pattern can contain poems of joy. Sonnets are good choices, or sonnet-length free verse poems or haikus. Walt Whitman's exuberant long lines can work well.

Nature poems are often exuberant and deserve their own chapter. Some of the other categories of joyful poetry are: food, religions, and mystical transcendence, to name a few.

Food Poetry

Related to nature poems are food poems. This is where the natural world transforms into nourishment for bodies: in meals. William Stafford, a good Kansan by birth and upbringing, understood the food cycle from farm to table. He begins this poem with "Sudden," and then travels from earth to sky, and from isolation to community:

Ode to Garlic by William Stafford
Sudden, it comes for you
in the cave of yourself where you know
and are lifted by important events.

Say you are dining and it happens:
Soaring like an eagle, you are
pierced by a message from the midst of life:

Memory—what holds the days together—touches
your tongue. It is from deep in the earth
and it reaches out kindly, saying, "Hello Old Friend."
It makes alike, all offspring of powerful
forces, part of one great embrace of democracy,
united across every boundary.
You walk out generously, giving it back

in a graceful wave, what you've been given.
Like a child, you breathe on the world, and it shines.

The brain's olfactory center, connected to the brain's limbic system, can retrieve memories quickly. Garlic is so strong that it is memory itself. It has an earthiness, "from deep in the earth," and the taster becomes an eagle, beyond gravity. The narrator moves from isolation to social unity. The exuberance of the poem is in these contrasts and exaggerations. The garlic clove becomes "part of one great embrace of democracy." Stafford uses the term "ode" to suggest the public celebration—the poem was written for a garlic festival—but it is a brief ode, and joyous.
My own poem celebrates gourmand joys with a group of friends:

> **Friday Nights, by Denise Low**
> One time the plattered pig,
> with Farrah eating the eyes,
> Roger the cheeks and ears,
> and the rest of us the limbs.
>
> Another time we consumed
> Arvin's hand-raised steer
> diced, marinated and offered
> like a blood sacrifice.
> In spring, we ate morels whole—
> smoky and wild labyrinths—
> emissaries from the Underworld
> sautéed in butter and wine.
>
> We talked, yes, and drank wine
> as we chewed forests and meadows
> seas and reefs—
> as we became one flesh.

Religious Joy
One of the turning points in my life was reading Allen Ginsberg's poem "Kaddish" when I was nineteen. Most of the poem has a Whitmanesque, rolling cadence, but some sections are especially lyrical and hymn-like, like "Hymmnn," which begins: "In the world which He has created according to his will Blessed Praised." The entire poem is online at Academy of American Poets.

The term "Kaddish" refers to a Jewish remembrance prayer for the dead. Ginsberg hybridizes this Hebrew form with free verse to express mixed emotions for his mother's difficult life and death. The exclamation marks, the parallel structure, the repetitions—all create an emotional rather than narrative reading experience. Once I heard Ginsberg read this poem, at high volume, and how powerful it was. Juxtaposition of his mother Naomi's mental illness with the "blessed be" praises creates an exuberant mood, despite the grief.

I grew up in independent congregation of the Congregational Church. The hymns were unlike anything I heard during the rest of the week. Their simple rhythms and repetitions underlie my unconscious understanding of poetry. The Christian writer Gerard Manley Hopkins wrote in this religious genre most of his career, in poems that are complex hymns like this one:

As Kingfishers Catch Fire, by Gerard Manley Hopkins
As kingfishers catch fire, dragonflies draw flame;
As tumbled over rim in roundy wells
Stones ring; like each tucked string tells, each hung bell's
Bow swung finds tongue to fling out broad its name;
Each mortal thing does one thing and the same:
Deals out that being indoors each one dwells;
Selves — goes itself; myself it speaks and spells,
Crying Whát I dó is me: for that I came.

I say móre: the just man justices;
Keeps grace: thát keeps all his goings graces;
Acts in God's eye what in God's eye he is —
Christi — for Christ plays in ten thousand places,
Lovely in limbs, and lovely in eyes not his
To the Father through the features of men's faces.

Hopkins begins with nature and shifts to orthodoxy of Christian terms of "grace," "Christ," and "God's eye," but not biblical law. The quiet joy of this poem is the beauty of natural and spiritual order. The single, "mortal thing" contrasts with the "ten thousand" in the religious realm.

The most specific religious poems of joy are Psalms. The Old Testament has a book devoted to direct address of the Lord. Some are laments, and some rejoice.

The last stanza of the hymn "Awake, My Soul, and with the Sun" is used as a doxology. Words are by Thomas Ken, written in 1674. The music is older, 1551, and attributed to Louis Bourgeois. The repetitions, parallel structure, rhythm, rhyme, and content are equal sides of a geometrical symmetry made of words:

> Praise God, from whom all blessings flow;
> Praise Him, all creatures here below;
> Praise Him above, ye heavenly host;
> Praise Father, Son, and Holy Ghost.

These verses, accompanied by chorus of a congregation and an organ, resound beautifully. The content of the verse reflects Psalm 8, review of the cosmos. It uses parallelism common among oral literary traditions:

> **Psalm 8 (King James translation)**
> O Lord, our Lord, how excellent is thy name in all the earth! who hast set thy glory above the heavens.
> Out of the mouth of babes and sucklings hast thou ordained strength because of thine enemies, that thou mightest still the enemy and the avenger.
> When I consider thy heavens, the work of thy fingers, the moon and the stars, which thou hast ordained;
> What is man, that thou art mindful of him? and the son of man, that thou visitest him?
> For thou hast made him a little lower than the angels, and hast crowned him with glory and honour.
> Thou madest him to have dominion over the works of thy hands; thou hast put all things under his feet:
> All sheep and oxen, yea, and the beasts of the field;
> The fowl of the air, and the fish of the sea, and whatsoever passeth through the paths of the seas.
> O Lord our Lord, how excellent is thy name in all the earth!

The parallelism, repetitions, direct address of "O Lord, our Lord," catalogue of the cosmos—all these create a spell-like quality as it is recited or sung.

The Mystic's Joy

The most profound joy in the poet's lexicon is spiritual, or *agape* in Greek. Poetry is the genre that most ably describes the mystic's experience of transcendence. Maybe some visual artists come close, like William Blake, who uses words along with images. The description of mystical joy begins with release from physical laws, as well as orthodox religion. Rumi describes going into a state of "no religion, no blasphemy" in this mystical moment:

Last Night by Rumi
Last night,
I saw the realm of joy and pleasure.
There I melted like salt;
no religion, no blasphemy,
no conviction or uncertainty remained.
In the middle of my heart,
a star appeared,
and the seven heavens were lost in its brilliance.

Multiplicity and duality reduce into one single, unified vision, a "star," whose light overwhelms the "seven heavens." This is sublime joy. The poem needs only a few lines to create its impact.

One of the most translated haiku is Basho's "Frog in an Old Pond." Most end with "sound of water" in various forms, but Alan Watts's ending is my favorite:

The old pond,
A frog jumps in:
Plop!

The sound joins human and frog worlds into one joyous moment.

Linda Rodriguez begins with a love poem that she transforms, in the end, to something much larger:

How to Be Alone in Love by Linda Rodriguez
Hold fast, first.
Continue to give,
even when no one wants
what you offer. The power, the wonder
is in the giving.
Call yourself out of yourself,
Shedding old skins.
Stripping bare to organ and bone,
open the heart's vein
and give your blood. Commit
and continue to commit.
These choices are always yours.

Be love's fool.
Become God's.
He will understand.
He too loved immoderately.

The sounds, the repetitions of words, the turning and returning to the theme of "Be love's fool" is like the emotion of the spurned lover. The shift to spiritual love is unexpected, but logical, sequence. This is beautifully crafted to fit content to form.

Techniques for Joyful Poetry
- Use direct, Anglo Saxon-based vocabulary—like Hopkins, for example.
- Maintain a consistent, heightened diction through slight hyperbole and/or repetition and/or detailed description.
- Transcend physical boundaries of the moment.
- Show movement from start to the ending.
- Avoid sentimentality, clichés, vague generalities, and lax writing.

A pitfall of writing about an upbeat mood is the temptation to write platitudes that have superficial gloss rather than substantive, earned joy. The pejorative term "greeting card verse" refers to the quick abstractions that take little thought. Sentimentality is a cute puppy photograph. It is a giant red valentine. Sentimentality is an extreme form of cliché.

American poetry of the 20th-21st century has a strain of earnestness that can veer into sentimentality. Experimental poetry—with its erosion of syntax, its mix of media, its investigations—is a reaction against simplistic awe. Heavy metal rock, similarly, is a reaction to teen-love 1960s popular music that can be insipid.

I believe joyful poetry is worth the risk.

Suggestions for Your Writing
- Choose a favorite food and describe it in detail. Set aside that page, remember the details, and write that food's poem. Try for two or three stanzas, with a pivot in the middle or near the end.
- Remember a joyful moment of your life. Write a poem about the setting of that moment—this oblique approach can help you avoid sentimentality or vague descriptions.

⊕ Write about music. Trying to describe this system of sounds on paper will challenge you. Joy, like music, is beyond two-dimensional, tallying description.

More Poems of Joy

Recuerdo by Edna St. Vincent Millay
We were very tired, we were very merry—
We had gone back and forth all night on the ferry.
It was bare and bright, and smelled like a stable—
But we looked into a fire, we leaned across a table,
We lay on a hill-top underneath the moon;
And the whistles kept blowing, and the dawn came soon.

We were very tired, we were very merry—
We had gone back and forth all night on the ferry;
And you ate an apple, and I ate a pear,
From a dozen of each we had bought somewhere;
And the sky went wan, and the wind came cold,
And the sun rose dripping, a bucketful of gold.

We were very tired, we were very merry,
We had gone back and forth all night on the ferry.
We hailed, "Good morrow, mother!" to a shawl-covered head,
And bought a morning paper, which neither of us read;
And she wept, "God bless you!" for the apples and pears,
And we gave her all our money but our subway fares.

Honky Tonk in Cleveland, Ohio by Carl Sandburg
It's a jazz affair, drum crashes and cornet razzes.
The trombone pony neighs and the tuba jackass snorts.
The banjo tickles and titters too awful.
The chippies talk about the funnies in the papers.
   The cartoonists weep in their beer.
   Ship riveters talk with their feet
    To the feet of floozies under the tables.
A quartet of white hopes mourn with interspersed snickers:
    "I got the blues.
    I got the blues.
    I got the blues."
And . . . as we said earlier:
   The cartoonists weep in their beer.

Fierce Heart by Stephen Meats
In the field across the street
patches of snow are lacunae
in the solid world
the eye tries to, but can't fill in.
A flock of feeding starlings
pleats and folds
among clumps of grass
the sun draws up
through the snow.
Suddenly a whisper
of translucent wings
and the starlings rise together.
In every mote
of that cloud undulating
across the white sky
a fierce heart beating
200 times a minute.

Excursion by Caleb Puckett
Shrewd blue eyes survey the splintered, the cratered, the smoldering—
the manic crosshatching of limbs, stumps and stray bits of machinery—
catching, however inadvertently, the remnants of some songbird
scattered across the black slur of forest floor.

It's the décor of a summer picnic, the accoutrements of romance,
the view of ground zero many klicks away from that first big kiss.

Basho. "Old Frog in a Pond," trans. Alan Watts. *Poem Hunter*.
-----. "Tis the First Snow," trans. W. G. Aston. *History of Japanese Lit.,* 1899.
Low, Denise. "Friday Nights." *New and Selected Poems*, 2nd. Penthe, 2007. 48.
Meats, Stephen. *Dark Dove Descending*. Mammoth, 2013. 14
Puckett, Caleb. "Excursion." *Fate Lines / Desire Lines*. Mammoth 2014. 54.
Rodriguez, Linda. *Heart's Migration: Poems*. Tia Chucha Press, 2009. 136.
Rumi, "Rumi Odes and Quatrains," Shahram Shiva, trans. *Rumi Network*.
Stafford, William. "Ode to Garlic." *Ask Me*. Graywolf, 2014. 84.

AWE

The definition of the word "awe" is more complex than the slangy "awesome"; it is "a feeling of reverential respect mixed with fear or wonder" (Merriam Webster). Fear spikes the emotional impact of awe: Tornados inspire awe. The copperhead snake in my garden evokes awe. The cute kitten pictures on Facebook do not inspire true awe.

Awe is one of the most difficult moods for 21st century writers. The World Wars, the Cold War, terrorism, Internet deception, politics—these make people wary. Cynicism is a default response.

A further risk, at the other extreme of awe, like with poetry of joy, is sentimentality. The cast of Graeco-Roman gods is trivialized by clichéd appearances in 19th century doggerel. Still, poets write about awe, and often the gods appear, disguised in various garbs. Awe suggests the divine.

Awe as a genre is a distilled form, short and sweet. Practitioners of awe-filled writing need control of all the writer's tricks.

The Short Lyric Poem and Awe

The short lyric, or the lyrical prose poem, is most closely aligned to the content of awe. Lyrical poetry is about creating intense responses in readers. Poets must appeal to spirit, thought, emotion, and the body to create this magic. Physical appeal is primary, before awe-filled transcendence. Although people are burdened with abstract thought, we also have sensory sections of our brains, what Robert Bly calls the "reptile brain," which connects to unconscious bodily functions. So, the poet is a snake charmer, trying to lure readers' inner reptiles into the poem's trance. A poem's repetitions—repeated sounds, cadence, and pacing—all add to the mood. The essential quality of lyric is internal rhythm, enacted by the line breaks. Indeed, the basic difference between poetry and prose, simply, is line breaks. So, the very first choice a poet makes is what kind of lines to use. Five-stress lines like Shakespeare dramas? No line breaks for prose poetry? Short lines for immediacy?

Frederick Turner and Ernst Poppel, researchers of global poetry line lengths, find that short lines are more quickly absorbed. People process clumps of words with pauses for comprehension: "A listener will absorb about three seconds of heard speech without pause or reflection, then stop listening briefly to integrate and make sense of what he has heard" (296). Most people need .3 of a second to process language. This pause is the line break. Turner and Poppel measured Latin, Greek, English, Chinese, Japanese, French, Zambian, New Guinea Eipo, Slavic and Celtic poetic lines (286). The three-second interval is consistent, about 2.5 seconds for lyric poetry lines and about 3.5 seconds for epic lines. The most apt lines for the mood of awe are short ones.

Lyrical Poems of Awe

Many poems have awe as a theme. Harley Elliott's short lyric of eighteen lines has beauty, surprise, and a kick at the end:

Butterfly Master, by Harley Elliott
This butterfly stopping on my cheek
would choose yours too
if you had fallen down among
grass and pasture flowers
and your face closed
hard as mine.

This small hinged mosaic
of orange black and palomino
has been given a name
and the danger of names hovers
close to both of us today.
Walking up   it stops at
the doorway of my eye:
there I am
blinded by words
in the shining light of its face.
We rush together
earth and sky.

"Butterfly Master" illustrates the brevity, the intensity of image, and the risk inherent in a person's immersion into nature. The "fear" aspect of awe's definition appears in Elliott's words "danger," "blinded," and "rush." The word "palomino" suggests the wild bronco ride of the poem. Shifts of scale are Elliott's genius here—especially the last stanza where the fragile, small butterfly and the narrator both must face the immensity of temporal and spatial eternity. The poem makes them equals. Short lines in the ending couplet emphasize this implosion of the hierarchy that puts humans within nature. This is a dangerous—and wonderful—place.

Here is a more ambivalent response to nature's might in this prose poem by Diane Glancy:

Petrified Forest National Park by Diane Glancy
A bird flew from the ditch, hit the windshield with a loud click where I drove. I *winged* it. Someone leaving. The threat of snow. It is only the voice of birds. Knife City I pass by the road.

Here nature arrives from the "ditch," and the narrator's car kills it. This is no romantic view. Birds' origins are in the time of dinosaurs—the time of the Petrified Forest. This setting is a background thrum. Themes of "threat," passing ("Someone leaving") and disembodied birds make this a snapshot of decay. The final sentence, about the retail outlet named "Knife City" (near Holbrook, Arizona), makes the narrator also another passer-by. This is a bleak poem that responds, like Elliott's poem, to the larger scale of time and nature. This is a dark side of awe.

Lyrical Practicum:

Short lyric poetry expresses, foremost, emotions, more than any other genre. To achieve this word-package of dynamite, the following are important considerations:

- ⊕ Brevity. A lyric is shorter, like a fourteen-line sonnet. The brevity makes it possible to sustain heightened emotion.
- ⊕ Compression. Because the lyric literary work is short, it must be highly compressed. Details are carefully chosen to telegraph information in a few images. Synecdoche, a part of something referring to the whole, is important here—like "silver-back gorilla" or simply "silver-back" is shorthand for a powerful, older leader. Metonymy substitutes one object or idea for another. "The White House" is an associated building that means the United States presidency.
- ⊕ Parables, fables, and oral-tradition tales are good models for poets, because they reduce details to basics.
- ⊕ Intimate point of view. First-person narration occurs in the first Sappho's 8th century B.C.E. verse. The first person "I" creates a feeling of immediate conversation. The speaker is a reliable guide, sympathetic, observant, omniscient—having knowledge of past and future. Third person— "she/he/it," "they," "one"—and second person

- Unity is the lyricist's goal, in form and content—refrains, repeated motifs (a single color as in "Butterfly Master" by Harley Elliott) and diction. Consistent rhythm, sound patterns, vocabulary, line lengths, theme and other essentials of unity are most important for lyrical impact. No anomalies should slow down a poem.
- Rhythm. A pulse goes through a good poem, like a powwow drum keeps a heartbeat going throughout a dance. Rhythm is part of the repetition that charms reptile brains.
- Intensity. In writing, intensity comes from (1) striking images, (2) abbreviated, dramatic stories, (3) compression of time (hyperfocus on a few moments), (4) extremes of vocabulary, (5) dramatic climax, (6) surprising turns.
- Revelations. Discoveries of the intimate, reliable narrator are readers' epiphanies. These are momentous. Dante Rossetti called a lyrical sonnet "a moment's monument." This micro-examination, ideally, creates memorable, life-changing shifts of perception.

These are tools of awe. The short lyric poem is arrival of a locomotive train. The station platform shudders. Sights blur and the roar overcomes every other sound. Words fail—almost.

Suggestions for Your Writing:
- Make a list of experiences that made you feel awe. Choose one and write a poem of no more than fourteen lines.
- After writing the fourteen-line poem, write one of twenty-four.
- Think of one of the most momentous days of your life. Birth of a child? First romance? First view of a mountain or ocean? Write a poem that includes six sound adjectives about it (or smells, tastes, textures, colors).
- Go to a museum and walk the galleries until you find an amazing exhibit or painting. Write about it.

More Poems of Awe

Behind Me — dips Eternity - by Emily Dickinson

Behind Me — dips Eternity -
Before Me — Immortality -
Myself — the Term between -
Death but the Drift of Eastern Gray,
Dissolving into Dawn away,
Before the West begin -
'Tis Kingdoms — afterward — they say -
In perfect — pauseless Monarchy -
Whose Prince — is Son of None -
Himself — His Dateless Dynasty -
Himself — Himself diversify -
In Duplicate divine -
'Tis Miracle before Me — then -
'Tis Miracle behind — between -
A Crescent in the Sea -
With Midnight to the North of Her -
And Midnight to the South of Her -
And Maelstrom — in the Sky -

from *Holy Sonnets* by John Donne

Batter my heart, three-person'd God, for you
As yet but knock, breathe, shine, and seek to mend;
That I may rise and stand, o'erthrow me, and bend
Your force to break, blow, burn, and make me new.
I, like an usurp'd town to another due,
Labor to admit you, but oh, to no end;
Reason, your viceroy in me, me should defend,
But is captiv'd, and proves weak or untrue.
Yet dearly I love you, and would be lov'd fain,
But am betroth'd unto your enemy;
Divorce me, untie or break that knot again,
Take me to you, imprison me, for I,
Except you enthrall me, never shall be free,
Nor ever chaste, except you ravish me.

Alone and Drinking under the Moon by Li Po
Amongst the flowers I
am alone with my pot of wine
drinking by myself; then lifting
my cup I asked the moon
to drink with me, its reflection
and mine in the wine cup, just
the three of us; then I sigh
for the moon cannot drink,
and my shadow goes emptily along
with me never saying a word;
with no other friends here, I can
but use these two for company;
in the time of happiness, I
too must be happy with all
around me; I sit and sing
and it is as if the moon
accompanies me; then if I
dance, it is my shadow that
dances along with me; while
still not drunk, I am glad
to make the moon and my shadow
into friends, but then when
I have drunk too much, we
all part; yet these are
friends I can always count on
these who have no emotion
whatsoever; I hope that one day
we three will meet again,
deep in the Milky Way.

Elliott, Harley. *Darkness at Each Elbow.* Hanging Loose Press, 1993.
Glancy, Diane. *It Was Then: Diagram of the Elemental.* Mammoth Publications, 2012. 59.
Li Po. "Alone and Drinking under the Moon." *Poet Seers.* Accessed 28 Aug. 2017.
Turner, Frederick and Ernst Poppel, "The Neural Lyre: Poetic Meter, the Brain, and Time" (*Poetry,* Aug. 1983: 277-309). 286.

CELEBRATION AND ODES

Odes are long, formal poems derived from Greek literary tradition. They vary in form. Content often infers a more public audience rather than an individual respondent (in contrast to sonnets). Originally, they celebrated victorious athletes, political figures, or public events—so the more communal intention for this poem remains. Odes are often dedicated to someone or some place.

Odes depend on repetitions of rhythm, meter, and/or meaning to emphasize emotion over a longer duration of time. However, they do not have set length, meter or rhyme scheme. "Ode" comes from the Greek word *aeidein,* meaning to sing or to chant, which indicates its connection to lyricism. Odes have a long history in Latin and English literary traditions.

PINDARIC ODES

To discuss odes, a few Greek terms are helpful. Do skip this history if details of Greek origins are not of interest.

Pindar (552–442 B.C.E), born in Thebes, is credited with creating the ode form. He lived during the height of Greek verse drama. Odes were originally sung as choral works to praise a hero. A family might commission the poem for formal public festivities. The Poetry Foundation defines the Pindaric ode as "a public poem, set to music that celebrated athletic victories."

The Athenian Greek chorus sang or chanted odes in unison, with musical accompaniment of an aulos (wooden recorder or flute) or lyre. Movements of the chorus parallel the ode's structure:

- ⊕ Strophe: "Turn" in Greek. The part of an ancient Greek choral ode sung (and danced) by the chorus when moving from east to west, or to the right of the center, where they conclude this portion.
- ⊕ Antistrophe: "Turning back." This counter-turn is the second part of an ode, performed after the chorus makes a turn and moves from west to east, or to the left of the center (sometimes an altar).
- ⊕ Epode: The stand or conclusion to a choral ode, sung from the center. Here the chorus halts and faces the audience to emphasize the ending. The epode finds a middle ground for the two opposite points of view of

the strophe and antistrophe. This is based on the common Greek rhetorical construction, "On the one hand this…, and on the other hand, that." The epode is the balancing out of two opposite directions. This remains important.

Pindar's ode is a patterned poem of three parts corresponding to the movements of the chorus: (1) strophe, an original and complex poetic structure, created by the poet; (2) antistrophe, a section that mirrors the first section in form; (3) a concluding stanza, the epode, in a different stanzaic form. Stanzas could be four to thirty lines.

English language Pindaric odes are less theatrical, but they still follow the form of Pindar's odes. "The Progress of Poesy" by Thomas Gray is a famous Pindaric ode, as well as William Wordsworth's "Ode on Intimations of Immortality." Wordsworth's long, autobiographical ode gains mythic context by use of this form. These first stanzas illustrate his strophe/antistrophe pattern:

Ode on Intimations of Immortality
by William Wordsworth
I
There was a time when meadow, grove, and stream,
The earth, and every common sight,
To me did seem
Apparelled in celestial light,
The glory and the freshness of a dream.
It is not now as it hath been of yore;
Turn whereso'er I may,
By night or day,
The things which I have seen I now can see no more.
II
The rainbow comes and goes,
And lovely is the rose,
The Moon doth with delight
Look round her when the heavens are bare;
Waters on a starry night
Are beautiful and fair;
The sunshine is a glorious birth;
But yet I know, where'er I go,
That there hath past away a glory from the earth. . ..

SAPPHIC ODES

The ode attributed to Sappho (born in Lesbos between 630 and 612 BCE) is composed of irregular quatrains (four-line stanzas). Her eponymous form is derived from the Aeolian tradition (along with the Aeolian harp). She begins an ode "To Aphrodite":

Sappho 1
Mind shimmering, deathless Aphrodite,
Child of Zeus, weaver of wiles,
I beg you, do not crush my spirit
with anguish, Lady,

but come here now, if ever before
you heard my voice in the distance
and heeded my prayer, left your father's
golden house,

yoked your chariot pulled by sparrows
swift and beautiful over the black earth,
their wings a blur as they streaked from heaven
through the middle air— . . . (translated Stanley Lombardo)

The first three lines of each stanza start an emphatic pattern (accent on first words, often) that the fourth undercuts with a quick finish. Academy of American Poets notes emotion of this ode: "The strict meter of the sapphic, with its starts and stops, creates a powerful emotion."

"Sapphics" by Algernon Charles Swinburne is a long ode that uses this form. He imitates the original Greek line accents (syllables 1, 5, and 10). Each stanza has three longer lines and a fourth short line to conclude. This is the beginning of the poem:

Sapphics by Algernon Charles Swinburn
All the night sleep came not upon my eyelids,
Shed not dew, nor shook nor unclosed a feather,
Yet with lips shut close and with eyes of iron
   Stood and beheld me.

Then to me so lying awake a vision
Came without sleep over the seas and touched me,
Softly touched mine eyelids and lips; and I too,
   Full of the vision,

Saw the white implacable Aphrodite,
Saw the hair unbound and the feet unsandalled
Shine as fire of sunset on western waters;
   Saw the reluctant

Feet, the straining plumes of the doves that drew [her,
Looking always, looking with necks reverted,
Back to Lesbos, back to the hills whereunder
   Shone Mitylene;

Heard the flying feet of the Loves behind her
Make a sudden thunder upon the waters,
As the thunder flung from the strong unclosing
   Wings of a great wind.

HORACE'S ODES

The Horatian ode (or Latin ode), named for the Roman poet who was born about 65 B.C.E., is less formal and suggests reflection more than public proclamation. It is not designed for the theater. This poem shows general reflection on love, in these opening two stanzas:

To Venus by Horace
O Venus, the queen of Cnidos and Paphos,
spurn your beloved Cyprus, and summoned
by copious incense, come to the lovely shrine
of my Glycera.

And let that passionate boy of yours, Cupid,
and the Graces with loosened zones, and the Nymphs,
and Youth, less lovely without you, hasten here,
and Mercury too.

In Horatian odes (in the original Latin) the end word of every line in the stanza rhymes with alternate lines in that stanza. English language odists follow this tradition. The more tranquil mood of a Horatian ode is reflected in evenly balanced stanzas, as illustrated by John Keats's "To a Nightingale," which begins:

My heart aches, and a drowsy numbness pains
My sense, as though of hemlock I had drunk,
Or emptied some dull opiate to the drains
One minute past, and Lethe-wards had sunk. . ..

Although this type of ode extends through many stanzas, the three parts—strophe, antistrophe, and epode—are clear progressions.

IRREGULAR ODES

Romantic English poets revived the ode tradition and developed it into one of their main forms. The key is the "turn" and resolution of two opposite directions. John Keats, Percy Bysshe Shelley, and others used regular rhyme and rhythm schemes, while William Wordsworth combined different prosody in his extended "Ode on the Intimations of Immortality"—made up of long and short lines, epigrams, and more direct statements. Wordsworth anticipated Walt Whitman's long, unfurling lines. The irregular ode retains both the tone and the thematic elements of the classical odes as well as their formal structures, but it is not exclusively Pindaric or Horatian.

ENGLISH ODES

Keats is one of the practitioners of this uniquely English variation of irregular odes. Usually, the English ode is iambic (stress on the second syllable). Stanzas have ten lines—a quatrain and a sestet (4 + 6). This regularity gives a more solid foundation to the dynamic three-part structure of the ode. Keats's "Ode on a Grecian Urn" illustrates the three sections of an English ode, arranged to the poet's own plan, but restrained within a regular pattern. Here, the silent, unmoving *objet d'art* of the strophe contrasts to the lively painted scene upon it (antistrophe). The final epode combines both strands into a final, integrated image. Look for more emphatic moments at intervals within this longer poem:

Ode on a Grecian Urn by John Keats
Thou still unravish'd bride of quietness,
  Thou foster-child of Silence and slow Time,
Sylvan historian, who canst thus express
  A flowery tale more sweetly than our rhyme:
What leaf-fringed legend haunts about thy shape
  Of deities or mortals, or of both,
    In Tempe or the dales of Arcady?
  What men or gods are these? what maidens loth?
What mad pursuit? What struggle to escape?
  What pipes and timbrels? What wild ecstasy?
Heard melodies are sweet, but those unheard
  Are sweeter; therefore, ye soft pipes, play on;

Not to the sensual ear, but, more endear'd,
  Pipe to the spirit ditties of no tone:
Fair youth, beneath the trees, thou canst not leave
  Thy song, nor ever can those trees be bare;
    Bold lover, never, never canst thou kiss,
Though winning near the goal--yet, do not grieve;
    She cannot fade, though thou hast not thy bliss,
      For ever wilt thou love, and she be fair!

Ah, happy, happy boughs! that cannot shed
  Your leaves, nor ever bid the Spring adieu;
And, happy melodist, unwearied,
  For ever piping songs for ever new;
More happy love! more happy, happy love!
  For ever warm and still to be enjoy'd,
    For ever panting, and for ever young;
All breathing human passion far above,
  That leaves a heart high-sorrowful and cloy'd,
    A burning forehead, and a parching tongue.

Who are these coming to the sacrifice?
  To what green altar, O mysterious priest,
Lead'st thou that heifer lowing at the skies,
  And all her silken flanks with garlands drest?
What little town by river or sea shore,
  Or mountain-built with peaceful citadel,
    Is emptied of this folk, this pious morn?
And, little town, thy streets for evermore
  Will silent be; and not a soul to tell
    Why thou art desolate, can e'er return.

O Attic shape! Fair attitude! with brede
  Of marble men and maidens overwrought,
With forest branches and the trodden weed;
  Thou, silent form, dost tease us out of thought
As doth eternity: Cold pastoral!
  When old age shall this generation waste,
    Thou shalt remain, in midst of other woe
Than ours, a friend to man, to whom thou say'st,
  'Beauty is truth, truth beauty'--that is all
    Ye know on earth, and all ye need to know.

Keats punctuates this longer, descriptive poem with memorable lines like the ending. "O Attic shape," the term of address, echoes the very beginnings of lyric poetry, in the same phrasing as an appeal to the Muse.

CONTEMPORARY ODES

Contemporary American poets do not always use the homogenous stanza patterns of Romantic irregular odists, but they may. The essentials of the ode for contemporary writers are the strophe-antistrophe-epode movement, even if this is embedded rather than overt. The tone and topics are more informal. According to Benna Crawford, "Contemporary odes may be humorous, sarcastic, or romantic and, occasionally, hark back to the structural origins of the form." A look at titles shows the range of subject matter and form: Pablo Neruda, "Ode to an Onion"; Lucille Clifton, "homage to my hips"; Alan Ginsberg, "Plutonium Ode"; Joy Harjo, "Perhaps the World Ends Here." Harjo's poem celebrates her kitchen table, which expands to become a larger social hub.

Writing Your Ode: Suggestions on Craft

- ⊕ The ode form usually is addressed to someone or something. The addressee may not be stated explicitly.
- ⊕ Stanza breaks help readers navigate a longer topic. Traditional odes have three to five long stanzas, most often. Like paragraphs written by lyric essayists, the poet breaks stanzas, when the topic changes.
- ⊕ A contemporary ode can be a discursive ramble. Lines and length depend on content.
- ⊕ Odes often use contrasts with counterturns, like Bach fugues.
- ⊕ The buildup to the conclusion creates drama, and the ending should reward that arc.
- ⊕ The ode makes a public statement or "complaint." It is a form that adapts to social commentary admirably.

Suggestions for Your Writing:
- ⊕ Go to your closet and choose a piece of clothing. Write an ode about it. Describe it thoroughly. Include any memories you have of occasions when you wore that article of clothing.
- ⊕ Choose one of the historic ode forms. Write an ode in that form. Then write the same poem in free verse.
- ⊕ Write an ode that commemorates a moment in history.

More Celebration Poems

Fan-Piece for Her Imperial Lord by Ezra Pound
O fan of white silk,
    clear as frost on the grass-blade,
You also are laid aside.

On Viewing the Skull and Bones of a Wolf by Alexander Posey
How savage, fierce and grim!
    His bones are bleached and white.
But what is death to him?
    He grins as if to bite.
He mocks the fate
    That bade, "Begone."
There's fierceness stamped
    In ev'ry bone.

Let silence settle from the midnight sky—
Such silence as you've broken with your cry;
The bleak wind howl, unto the ut'most verge
Of this mighty waste, thy fitting dirge.

Crawford, Benna. "Explanation of Odes." *Demand Media.* 28 April 2015
"Ode." *The Poetry Foundation.* Web. Accessed 23 Aug. 2017.
Prudchenko, Kate. "How Long Does an Ode Poem Have to Be?" *Demand Media.* 28 April 2015.
Sappho, trans. Stanley Lombardo. "Fragment 1." *Complete Poems and Fragments.* Hackett, 2016. 3.
Strand, Mark and Eavan Boland. *The Making of a Poem.* Norton, 2000.

REFLECTION AND ODES

In American poetry, the mood of reflection brings together many traditions. One is the Christian mode of religious self-examination, as in John Donne's works. Another is the pastoral tradition. The celebratory ode tradition is another. The contemporary American reflective poem draws on all of these.

The term "ode" has become a more general term for any poem longer than a sonnet but shorter than a long poem. The ode has evolved into a genre that can accommodate reflection and meditation. In contemporary writing, neither religious meditations nor pastorals have a set form, but they often have extended length.

Review of the narrator's moral state is a historic development after the Greeks. Nature poetry is a contemporary form that is developing along with concern with the ecology. Infinite variations are possible.

Self-Examination

In the novel *The Great Gatsby*, the tradition of religious reflection becomes a self-improvement list: "Rise from bed; dumbbell exercise and wall-scaling; study electricity; work; baseball and sports; practice elocution, poise, and how to attain it." Among the practical activities are the moral: "read one improving book or magazine per week and be better to parents." *The Autobiography of Benjamin Franklin* has similar lists. The individual is like a garden to be sown, weeded, and harvested. This extends into secular context the Christian process of self-examination and confession.

John Donne's poems often show this religious inclination, like this one:

Good Friday, 1613. Riding Westward by John Donne
Let man's Soul be a Sphere, and then, in this,
The intelligence that moves, devotion is,
And as the other Spheres, by being grown
Subject to foreign motion, lose their own,
And being by others hurried every day,
Scarce in a year their natural form obeys:
Pleasure or business, so, our Souls admit
For their first mover, and are whirled by it.
Hence is't, that I am carried towards the West
This day, when my Soules form bends toward the East.
There I should see a Sun, by rising set,

And by that setting endless day beget;
But that Christ on this Cross, did rise and fall,
Sin had eternally benighted all. . ..

    This illustrates the inner space created by a meditation, the "sphere," presented as a physical reality. The individual strives to improve his imperfect soul through the arc of the day and through a cycle of self-confession.
    Another John Donne poem, "Celestial Music" has many themes, including musical forms, and it includes a beloved. It also illustrates the mood of religious self-reflection, in a surprisingly contemporary way:

Celestial Music by John Donne
I have a friend who still believes in heaven.
Not a stupid person, yet with all she knows, she literally talks to God.
She thinks someone listens in heaven.
On earth she's unusually competent.
Brave too, able to face unpleasantness.

We found a caterpillar dying in the dirt, greedy ants crawling over it.
I'm always moved by disaster, always eager to oppose vitality
But timid also, quick to shut my eyes.
Whereas my friend was able to watch, to let events play out
According to nature. For my sake she intervened
Brushing a few ants off the torn thing, and set it down
Across the road.

My friend says I shut my eyes to God, that nothing else explains
My aversion to reality. She says I'm like the child who
Buries her head in the pillow
So as not to see, the child who tells herself
That light causes sadness—
My friend is like the mother. Patient, urging me
To wake up an adult like herself, a courageous person-

In my dreams, my friend reproaches me. We're walking
On the same road, except it's winter now;
She's telling me when you love the world you hear celestial music:
Look up, she says. When I look up, nothing.
Only clouds, snow, a white business in the trees
Like brides leaping to a great height—

> Then I'm afraid for her; I see her
> Caught in a net deliberately cast over the earth—
>
> In reality, we sit by the side of the road, watching the sun set;
> From time to time, the silence pierced by a birdcall.
> It's this moment we're trying to explain, the fact
> That we're at ease with death, with solitude.
> My friend draws a circle in dirt; inside, the caterpillar doesn't move.
> She's always trying to make something whole, something beautiful, an
>   [image
> Capable of life apart from her.
> We're very quiet. It's peaceful sitting here, not speaking. The
>   [composition
> Fixed, the road turning suddenly dark, the air
> Going cool, here and there the rocks shining and glittering—
> It's this stillness we both love.
> The love of form is a love of endings.

The ending is a true surprise, although the development of melancholy throughout the poem fits the end. The discursive stroll of the poem fits the theme of acceptance. What surprises me about Donne's poem is how, in form and in secular resolution, it foreshadows contemporary adaptations of the nature meditation. This minister—Dean of St. Paul's for the Church of England—turns not to Biblical scholarship, but to nature. His renouncement of form in the last lines foreshadows experimental poetry of later eras, in my humble opinion.

Donne lived on a relatively small island with greater homogeneity than the United States today or even today's England. *The Confessions of Saint Augustine* is not now common reading, as it was in Catholic days of England, nor are writings of Thomas More. Confession of faults is a private matter not often found in public discourse.

The Confessional school of poetry takes a personal point of view and applies it to domestic and other informal topics. Sylvia Plath examines herself in some detail in poems like "Daddy." Autobiographical details and self-analysis take the place of religious fervor.

Nonetheless, the mood of religious meditation remains, along with the assumption that an individual soul has importance. This contrasts to traditional American Indian literary forms, for examples, where poetry functions first as community expression.

In contemporary times, confessional, personal-examination poets must solve the problem of relevance to others to be effective.

Pastoral Reflection and Eco-Poetry

The pastoral tradition originated as "poetry that sought to imitate and celebrate the virtues of rural life" (Strand and Boland). Arcadia is a Greek region that became the idealized rural domicile in classical literature. It is the home of the Greek god Pan—god of the wilderness, mountains, and sheepherding. The name Pan comes from *paein,* "to pasture," direct ancestor of the term "pastoral." Authors of this genre are Hesiod (*Works and Days*), Theocritus, Virgil (*Eclogues*), Edmund Spenser, Philip Sidney ("The Old Arcadia"), and many more.

In pastoral works, the rural household is an idealized site of natural cycles under rule of human husbandry. In some cases, it becomes a parody of itself, as in pastoral court plays with courtesans dressed as shepherdesses. The form persisted into the 19th century, as "the Industrial Revolution replaced the court as a place from which to mourn for and celebrate rural life"; today it takes form in "laments about urban intrusion, celebrations of urban hubris, speculations about the future of the physical world, right up to the new eco-poetry" (Strand and Boland 208). Eco-poetry is a political and activist form of this lineage.

Jonathan Holden's poem about morel mushrooms exemplifies a contemporary approach to pastoralism:

Hunting for Morels by Jonathan Holden
Sometimes I think
if they were all around me
I would not see them—
that to elicit some
out of the shades of the ground
isn't technique like the rate
you walk or the middle distance
you guard with your faulty sight.
Maybe the man who goes empty-handed
after tramping miles of terrain
isn't ready to pick them out.
He carries with him
only half their name. The half
he needs—that other half

always on the tip of the tongue—
is a target he holds between his eyes
like the names of the women
that he once told he loved,
each name a landscape,
each warm head he had held
like an offering between
his hands, a breakable loaf,
their names his only proof
he had once walked through them—
though he may still remember
driving, his will aimed
at a small apartment, his heart
divided, the clocks in his wrists
striking, unable to stop.
Even then he may have known
he was too accurate.

Sometime, before I find them,
I could believe that if I go
empty-handed it would be because
I wanted restraint in my sight,
as if it were in my power to help
this earth, out of its ranges
of gray and this spongy generic
that tires the eyes
and where it is impossible
to be one thing at a time
pronounce their singular name
and plant morels in my path
to thumb me down
with their delicate shadowy thumbs.
Then the earth offers itself
to us anyway, all
its tender thumbs, the other
half of our words,
and we take whatever we see.

This quietly brilliant poem celebrates critical connection between human language and nature, "the other / half of our words." The poem begins (1) first-person perspective with observation of morels, (2) digresses into a memory in the middle, third-person "he," and then (3) returns to first-person reflection on the morels. This is the classic structure of a Greek ode, with synthesis at the end. The gentle terms for mushrooms, "tender thumbs," creates an idealized, pastoral vision of nature, with human-like "thumbs" that personify the fungus. The narrator negotiates between his inner associations—memory of a man and the women he "once loved"—and the outer finitude of the search for morels, creating a process of self-examination of human limits (from the religious examination tradition). Nature, not God, is the final arbiter.

Among the important practitioners of contemporary reflective nature poetry are Brenda Hillman, Jane Kenyon, Mary Oliver, Gary Snyder, Charles Wright, and many others. Edward Hirsch writes about future vigor of pastoralism, the "eco-feminist pastoralism." He includes Susan Griffin's *Women and Nature: The Roaring Inside Her* (1978). He notes how the anthology *Black Nature* (2010) "celebrates the overlooked tradition of African American nature poetry over four centuries." He envisions pastoralism as a direct lineage of ecological and activist poetry beyond current practices. The mannered French court enactments of idealized pastoralism have evolved into an activist politics of survival.

Variations: Contemporary Reflection Poems

Odes often fit with meditative moments. They are a loose enough form to accommodate reflections. They are not primarily narrative (a contrast to ballads, for example). Short lyric poems can make a more intense emotional impact; longer reflective poems, or odes, do not sustain that intensity, but they allow deeper exploration of a topic.

At the upper limit of length is the "long poem." Rachel Zucker examines the long poem on the Academy of American Poets website. She emphasizes opportunities of poems extended over three pages or more. Odes fall between sonnets and the long poem in length, but reflection can last as long as the poet can write.

The ode has, implied, a laudatory purpose, even if it may not be a public poem. It celebrates its subject: a nightingale (John Keats), the west wind (Percy Bysshe Shelley), the Confederate dead (Allen Tate), even socks (Pablo Neruda) and private body parts. Sharon Olds' book *Odes* contains reflection on the clitoris, the penis, a hip replacement, stretch marks, a trilobite, and dirt, to name a few.

Mood of a contemporary meditation is deepened by the diligent turning and re-turning toward the subject. Greg Field uses the extended length to write about mourning with indirection and a bit of narration:

Holding My Breath by Greg Field
Once I held my breath
under water for a year.
I looked up and concentrated
on the sun, its distorted disk
rippled on the water's surface.

I thought about the time
I was eight and dived
off our dock and held my breath
long enough to pull myself
below its fat fifty-gallon barrels.
Within the dock's hollow center,
I surfaced in shafts of sunlight
chopped by the lapping green water.

Over that year I watched months
sink heavy by my shoulders
followed by my love's blouses
and dresses waving by as they settled.

Next, black metal hangers like hooks,
baitless, cartwheeled down; passed
in front of my nose, bubbles drifted
from my nostrils, silver balloons of waste.

I looked up and saw them coming:
earrings, necklaces, bracelets, treasures
sinking through the liquid light.

Finally, the delicate translucence—
her ghost tumbled by, bubbles roiling
about its edges. I almost drew

a deep green breath, but my burned lungs
held as I settled deeper. I followed
the treasures of that life into darker water,
and cold mud where I dreamed—

> treading water under our dock's planking
> sucking in air, I became aware of the rust
> eating away the barrels' flaking sides
> and I saw that really, nothing floats.

This poem juxtaposes human-made items with nature. The jewelry and clothes from a lover, "my love's blouses" suspend in water as they suspend in time. After death, the objects remain. His title refers to the year of grief. He finally concludes, like Donne, that nature shapes the world, overriding any human experience— "nothing floats." He resolves the extended elegy with insights about a setting ruled by nature.

Writing the Reflection Poem: Techniques

- ⊕ Choose a topic worthy of your attention (and your audience's).
- ⊕ Begin with drama, enough to engage your readers. Strong language, images, topics—any of these can be an effective start.
- ⊕ Craft your narrative voice carefully. People often remember how a person speaks more than what the person says.
- ⊕ Become the mirror that reflects. Describe an object or idea objectively, and then complicate it with your associations.
- ⊕ The reflective poem, like the lyric essay, may use other rhetorical strategies, like stories, description, quotations, and dialogue.

Suggestions for Your Writing

- ⊕ Take one of your older, short poems. Read the original carefully and tease out three or more themes. Then write stanzas, one on each theme, using the original form. Voilà, an ode!
- ⊕ Sit outside for an hour and make a list of the natural elements—flora, fauna, rocks. Include the sky as well. Then compose an ode. Perhaps title it with the name of the place.
- ⊕ Sit outside in an urban setting. Make a list of what you observe, and repeat the process above, in terms that fit the city list.
- ⊕ Take a memory or history and describe it as fully as possible. Then look at other people involved; the setting; the impact on your own life. Use these as ways to extend the original description.

More Reflection Poems

The Wild Swans at Coole by W. B. Yeats
The trees are in their autumn beauty,
The woodland paths are dry,
Under the October twilight the water
Mirrors a still sky;
Upon the brimming water among the stones
Are nine and fifty swans.

The nineteenth Autumn has come upon me
Since I first made my count;
I saw, before I had well finished,
All suddenly mount
And scatter wheeling in great broken rings
Upon their clamorous wings.

I have looked upon those brilliant creatures,
And now my heart is sore.
All's changed since I, hearing at twilight,
The first time on this shore,
The bell-beat of their wings above my head,
Trod with a lighter tread.

Unwearied still, lover by lover,
They paddle in the cold,
Companionable streams or climb the air;
Their hearts have not grown old;
Passion or conquest, wander where they will,
Attend upon them still.

But now they drift on the still water
Mysterious, beautiful;
Among what rushes will they build,
By what lake's edge or pool
Delight men's eyes, when I awake some day
To find they have flown away?

Sheltered Garden by H.D.
I have had enough.
I gasp for breath.
Every way ends, every road,
every foot-path leads at last
to the hill-crest—
then you retrace your steps,
or find the same slope on the other side,
precipitate.
I have had enough—
border-pinks, clove-pinks, wax-lilies,
herbs, sweet-cress.
O for some sharp swish of a branch—
there is no scent of resin
in this place,
no taste of bark, of coarse weeds,
aromatic, astringent—
only border on border of scented pinks.
Have you seen fruit under cover
that wanted light—
pears wadded in cloth,
protected from the frost,
melons, almost ripe,
smothered in straw?
Why not let the pears cling
to the empty branch?
All your coaxing will only make
a bitter fruit—
let them cling, ripen of themselves,
test their own worth,
nipped, shriveled by the frost,
to fall at last but fair
With a russet coat.
Or the melon—
let it bleach yellow
in the winter light,
even tart to the taste—
it is better to taste of frost—
the exquisite frost—
than of wadding and of dead grass.
For this beauty,
beauty without strength,

chokes out life.
I want wind to break,
scatter these pink-stalks,
snap off their spiced heads,
fling them about with dead leaves—
spread the paths with twigs,
limbs broken off,
trail great pine branches,
hurled from some far wood
right across the melon-patch,
break pear and quince—
leave half-trees, torn, twisted
but showing the fight was valiant.
O to blot out this garden
to forget, to find a new beauty
in some terrible
wind-tortured place.

from The Book of a Monk's Life by Rainer Maria Rilke
I live my life in circles that grow wide
And endlessly unroll,
I may not reach the last, but on I glide
Strong pinioned toward my goal.

About the old tower, dark against the sky,
The beat of my wings hums,
I circle about God, sweep far and high
On through millenniums.

Am I a bird that skims the clouds along,
Or am I a wild storm, or a great song?

Dulce et Decorum Est by **Wilfred Edward Salter Owen**
Bent double, like old beggars under sacks,
Knock-kneed, coughing like hags, we cursed through sludge,
Till on the haunting flares we turned our backs,
And towards our distant rest began to trudge.
Men marched asleep. Many had lost their boots,
But limped on, blood-shod. All went lame, all blind;
Drunk with fatigue; deaf even to the hoots
Of gas-shells dropping softly behind.

Gas! GAS! Quick, boys! —An ecstasy of fumbling
Fitting the clumsy helmets just in time,
But someone still was yelling out and stumbling
And flound'ring like a man in fire or lime. —
Dim through the misty panes and thick green light,
As under a green sea, I saw him drowning.

In all my dreams before my helpless sight
He plunges at me, guttering, choking, drowning.

If in some smothering dreams, you too could pace
Behind the wagon that we flung him in,
And watch the white eyes writhing in his face,
His hanging face, like a devil's sick of sin,
If you could hear, at every jolt, the blood
Come gargling from the froth-corrupted lungs
Bitter as the cud
Of vile, incurable sores on innocent tongues, —
My friend, you would not tell with such high zest
To children ardent for some desperate glory,
The old Lie: *Dulce et decorum est*
Pro patria mori.

Field, Greg. *Black Heart.* Mammoth, 2014: 43-4.
Fitzgerald, Scott. *The Great Gatsby.* Charles Scribner's' Sons, 1925.
Hirsch, Edward. Academy of American Poets. Excerpted from *A Poet's Glossary* by Edward Hirsch, 2014. Accessed 4 Oct. 2017
Holden, Jonathan. *Glamour: Poems.* Mammoth, 2012: 13.
Rilke, Rainer Maria. "The Book of Hours." *Poems,* 1916. Translated by Jessie Lemont. Web.
Strand, Mark and Eavan Boland. *The Making of a Poem.* Norton, 2000. 208.
Zucker, Rachel. "An Anatomy of the Long Poem." *Academy of American Poets.*

BIOPHILIA— LOVE OF NATURE

When guided imagery leaders ask people to close their eyes, relax, and imagine an idyllic place, almost everyone chooses a natural landscape. Few choose Times Square. Imagining crystals, conch shells, pine cones, even abstracted geometric drawings will calm the mind. The human brain loves patterns. Poets are the masters of guided imagery, before New Age seekers coined the term. From the beginnings of the lyric in the Graeco-Roman tradition to the present, nature inspires poetry. The project is to make it new.

Biofilia, love of nature, is one of the oldest moods of verse. The term is from 1984 when Edward O. Wilson published his book *Biophilia*. He defines the term as "the urge to affiliate with other forms of life." Nature's patterns inspire. Many cultures connect deities to the overwhelming elements of nature: ocean, earth, rivers, lakes, mountains, thunderstorms. These all inspire biophilia.

Joy in Natural Objects

Emily Dickinson is but one poet who takes an object of nature and finds delight in describing it. She transcends the linear world of numbered snowflakes in this poem:

Snow Flakes by Emily Dickinson
I counted till they danced so
Their slippers leaped the town—
And then I took a pencil
To note the rebels down—
And then they grew so jolly
I did resign the prig—
And ten of my once stately toes
Are marshalled for a jig!

The tension between that finite, numbered, and serious beginning resolves with the ten toes joining in a "jig." Without really describing the snowflakes, she implies how joyous she became as the experience overcomes rational thought. The separation between nature and human dissolves.

English Romanticism

The Industrial Age brought urbanization, and a counter reaction to modernity was romanticism. William Wordsworth, in the late 1700s to early

1800s, celebrated the pastoral as industrialization destroyed it. His poem describes London as a naturalized scene:

Composed Upon Westminster Bridge, by William Wordsworth
Earth has not anything to show more fair:
Dull would he be of soul who could pass by
A sight so touching in its majesty:
This City now doth, like a garment, wear
The beauty of the morning; silent, bare,
Ships, towers, domes, theatres and temples lie
Open unto the fields, and to the sky;
All bright and glittering in the smokeless air.
Never did sun more beautifully steep
In his first splendor, valley, rock, or hill;
Ne'er saw I, never felt, a calm so deep!
The river glideth at his own sweet will:
Dear God! The very houses seem asleep;
And all that mighty heart is lying still!

In early morning, the air is "smokeless," and "houses seem asleep."
    The decline of the rural way of life leads to its idealization. Those of us a few generations from the farm (in 1900, 90% of the United States was rural) know from experience or family stories about the hardships of rural life. Those from sea-faring traditions know of drownings, storms, and hard labor of the sailor's and fisherman's life. Yet this 1817sonnet by Keats is about only beauty.

On the Sea, by John Keats
It keeps eternal whisperings around
Desolate shores, and with its mighty swell
Gluts twice ten thousand Caverns, till the spell
Of Hecate leaves them their old shadowy sound.
Often 'tis in such gentle temper found,
That scarcely will the very smallest shell
Be moved for days from where it sometime fell.
When last the winds of Heaven were unbound.

Oh, ye! who have your eyeballs vexed and tired,
Feast them upon the wideness of the Sea;
Oh ye! whose ears are dinned with uproar rude,
Or fed too much with cloying melody—
Sit ye near some old Cavern's Mouth and brood,
Until ye start, as if the sea nymphs quired!

"Quired" is archaic spelling of "choired." The Greek moon goddess Hecate adds a layer of deism and suggests the sublime. The poet is the reverent narrator who speaks in awed tones. The biophilia of "On the Sea" is clear. The human is dwarfed by the immensity of the ocean; is amplified by it; is inspired. The two-part structure is first description, with no human presence, then how to use the "Sea" as escape, a place to "brood." The description includes ways to suggest scale—waves are "ten thousand Caverns" and "the very smallest shell" is the opposite. The second half is about the human narrator and audience, including the traditional Greek salutation: "Oh, ye!" The two-part structure is non-human followed by humanization of nature.

NATURAL THEOLOGY

Animism, the idea that the world is alive and humans are not separate, is another way to approach biophilia. E Donald Two-Rivers (1941-2008) was a poet who used complex imagery of Ojibwe language:

Ode to a River by E. Donald Two-Rivers
Sitting on a river's edge.
watching sun rays dance
small wavelet to small wavelet—
Wah-she-kee-she-cook
the Indians call it.
Shade tree comforts me.
Gentle wind excites the air
to caress my brown face.
My breath is captured
by this river's humble majesty.

This spot where I repose
feels like a place
where spirits would dance and feast,
where time has preserved
a sense of mystery,

where harsh emotions
are released on quiet days.
Old campfire, deer trails to water's edge—
all confirm my thoughts.
This is a place where a small Indian boy
can sit dreaming big dreams.

Here time divides the poem into parts—present time, historic past, personal past, recent past (the "repose"). The first half is present tense, about the natural scene. It includes the Ojibwe term for "small wavelet" that is central to the poem. The second stanza moves into the past. The final couplet is about himself as a boy, past tense, transformed into present-tense time. He collapses time as he experiences nature.

Marianne Moore (1887-1972) is a poet known for her precise language and devotion to aesthetic details of nature, as in this poem:

The Fish by Marianne Moore
wade
through black jade.
    Of the crow-blue mussel-shells, one keeps
    adjusting the ash-heaps;
        opening and shutting itself like

an
injured fan.
    The barnacles which encrust the side
    of the wave, cannot hide
        there for the submerged shafts of the

sun,
split like spun
    glass, move themselves with spotlight swiftness
    into the crevices—
        in and out, illuminating

the
turquoise sea
    of bodies. The water drives a wedge
    of iron through the iron edge
        of the cliff; whereupon the stars,

> pink
> rice-grains, ink-
> > bespattered jelly fish, crabs like green
> > lilies, and submarine
> > > toadstools, slide each on the other.
>
> All
> external
> > marks of abuse are present on this
> > defiant edifice—
> > > all the physical features of
>
> ac-
> cident—lack
> > of cornice, dynamite grooves, burns, and
> > hatchet strokes, these things stand
> > > out on it; the chasm-side is
>
> dead.
> Repeated
> > evidence has proved that it can live
> > on what can not revive
> > > its youth. The sea grows old in it.

Moore creates an original form and breaks words to fit it, like "ac- / cident." The re-visioning of jelly fish, crabs, and other sea dwellers show a wide range of seascape. The narrator enters the world of her description. The last line blurs boundaries of time and place.

Tensions that energize any nature poem include binaries within nature and without; personal and universal; mortal and immortal; transient and eternal. The question of existence underlies writing of the biophilia poet.

Techniques for Nature Poems

- ⊕ Balance objective description with subjective commentary
- ⊕ Amp up your descriptive repertoire. Be sure to work with size, texture shape, color, and other five-sense dimensions
- ⊕ Think of your point-of-view as a camera lens; try close-up and distance settings for your poem.
- ⊕ Layer your poem with researched facts, blended in lyrically.

Suggestions for Your Writing

- ⊕ Write a celebration of a body of water that you know well. Or something that lives in it.
- ⊕ Situate yourself in a natural spot, in body or in mind. Think of its past and present. Braid the two in a poem.
- ⊕ Think of domesticated natural elements. Electricity of lightning is tamed and given wire pathways. Wood is lumber for shelves. Write a poem about one or more of these.

A Few More Nature Poems

A Jelly-Fish by Marianne Moore

Visible, invisible,
A fluctuating charm,
An amber-colored amethyst
Inhabits it; your arm
Approaches, and
It opens and
It closes;
You have meant
To catch it,
And it shrivels;
You abandon
Your intent—
It opens, and it
Closes and you
Reach for it—
The blue
Surrounding it
Grows cloudy, and
It floats away
From you.

Ts'ai Chi'h by Ezra Pound

The petals fall in the fountain,
    the orange coloured rose-leaves,
Their ochre clings to the stone.

Two-Rivers, E. Donald. *Powwows, Fatcats, and Indians.* Mammoth, 2003. 15.
Wilson Edward O. *Biophilia.* Harvard University Press, 1984.

ANGER

Anger is like infatuation. It hits quickly and flashes. However, anger is not an easy emotion to share. Words have the power to move audience members, and who wants a room full of enraged people?

Poetry can express all ranges of anger, from hot to cool. Duels in words by rappers is one stylized form, where name calling is developed to the highest degree. Performance poetry is often political, especially regarding personal identity in terms of ethnicity, gender, ageism, disability. Long-term anger, a slow burn, leads to satire.

In literary, or text-based, poetry, the topic of anger takes on many forms, most short in length. Danger of slander and libel arise, as anger can be directed at a person and result in legal action, if he or she can show damage. Most often, the offending party is not named directly.

Some of the techniques for writing angry poems include: hyperbole (exaggeration), details and facts, bitter humor, extended metaphors. The trick is to shape the purpose, especially the ending, to create a desired effect—a call to political action, perhaps. A warning against immoral behavior. Righteous outrage. The poet Luci Tapahonso begins every performance with a song and ends with a prayer or uplifting poem. She sometimes writes about the difficult history of *Diné* (Navajo) people often, but she always ends with hope. She models how justified anger has a place, but does not destroy.

Conflict generates literature. Anger points out problems to solve, through actions of characters in stories or resolutions of poems. Harnessing this energy can add drama. Naming problems can resolve anger and encourage reconciliation.

Jilted Lovers

This bitter poem builds as an abandoned lover cooks a meal alone instead part of a couple.

Puttanesca, by Michael Heffernan
Before I gave up wondering why everything
was a lot of nothing worth losing or getting back,
I took out a jar of olives, a bottle of capers,
a container of leftover tomato sauce with onions,
put a generous portion of each in olive oil

just hot enough but not too hot,
along with some minced garlic and a whole can of anchovies,
until the mixture smelled like a streetwalker's sweat,
then emptied it onto a half pound of penne, beautifully al dente,
under a heap of grated Pecorino Romano
in a wide bowl sprinkled with fresh chopped parsley.
If you had been there, I would have given you half,
and asked you whether its heavenly bitterness
made you remember anything you had once loved.

The ragged, sonnet-like verse uses the intense flavors of food and spices to amplify the narrator's feelings. The first two lines set up the failed relationship obliquely. It turns on the "streetwalker's sweat," which echoes the title, and it resolves with the final three lines that are bitter more than sweet.

Loss and Revenge

The oldest written work of European literary tradition is Homer's *Iliad*, which commences with anger. Achilles, the proud warrior is offended by Agamemnon and refuses to fight. The war evolves from the anger of Achilles. The epic is not entirely about anger, with its narratives and catalogues, but the parts that invoke anger are focused, heightened, and emotional:

The Iliad, Book 1: Invocation of the Muse, by Homer
Sing, Mountain Goddess, sing through me
That anger which most ruinously
Inflamed Achilles, Peleus' son,
And which, before the tale was done,
Had glutted Hell with champions—bold,
Stern spirits by the thousandfold;
Ravens and dogs their corpses ate.
            (Robert Graves, trans.)

Homer describes Achilles as "inflamed." Later, in the same book, Achilles himself speaks his anger:

The Iliad, Book 1, Homer by Homer
"... I vow
That all you Greeks assembled now
Before me—mark these words! —one day
Shall miss Achilles in the fray

And long for him, finding your chief
Incapable (despite all grief)
To save from Hector's murdering sword
Whole regiments; then at last, my lord,
Your anger inwards you shall turn,
Cursing the folly that dared spurn
Him who indignantly here speaks:
The best and bravest of all Greeks!"
                    (Robert Graves, trans.)

Notice his emphasis "mark these words." He uses the terms "vow" and "murdering sword" to express his anger. He uses the word "anger" itself. His last line is memorable, his own epithet. Epic poetry is mostly narrative, but along the way, high points like this discharge of anger keep audiences interested.

Political Satire

Anger can take the form of protest. Such works are often short and pithy, as this poem by African American writer Barry Barnes, written in the aftermath of the first Iraq conflict:

Taker of Limbs by Barry Barnes
How much for an arm?
How much for a leg?
Somewhere somehow, somebody will pay.
They will pay with sorrow. They will pay with grief.
And they will curse that damned war.
That damned war.
That damned thief.

Writers whose work is fueled by righteous anger include Langston Hughes, Josephine Miles, Rita Dove, Natasha Tretheway, Allen Ginsberg, Lucille Clifton, Adrian C. Louis, and many others.

The Fine Art of Insult

Insults are as old as poetry itself. Greeks, Romans, British, and Americans all find ways to sling the verbiage arrows. Walter Raleigh's epitaph for an enemy is sweet revenge indeed, the very last word(s):

Advertisement by Walter Raleigh
Here lies the noble Warrior that never blunted sword;
Here lies the noble Courtier that never kept his word;
Here lies his Excellency that governed all the state;
Here lies the Lord of Leicester that all the world did hate.

African Americans inherit a tradition of insult poetry, "playing the dozens," a competition of rhyming insults, often in performance. The classic opening is "Your mamma's so ugly ... ..." Rod Padgett writes this "is a hand-me-down from African slave ancestors." He notes one of the oldest African insult poems:

Anonymous
You really resemble
An old man who has no teeth
And who wants to eat elephant hide,

Or a woman without a backside
Who sits down on a hard wooden stool.

You also resemble a stupid dolt
Who while hunting lets an antelope pass by
And who knows that his father is sick at home.

Maryfrances Wagner uses anger as an unexpected ending to a nature poem. It shocks here, and it also sends readers back through the poem to reflect on the contrast between acceptance of nature's ways and violence against nature:

Black Snakes by Maryfrances Wagner
Through grass, the black snakes
thread. Iridescent scales

glint in sunlight. The pair flow
like water's wake across the patio

and into a chipmunk hole.
Thicker ribbons comb grass

when they emerge:
tape measures of darkness

curving around dogwood, over
flat stones, and into stacked kindling.

Within the week, the snakes undulate
through my neighbor's fescue.

By day's end he shoves across my fence
Their severed heads stuck in his rake.

A war of words may defuse further violence. Yet the example of Achilles shows how one man's anger, and his oratory, can start wars.

Strategies for Angry Writings

- ⊕ Titles save explanations. "Divorce" or "Triangle" explains a lot.
- ⊕ Set up the poem with brief narrative or imagery, not abstractions.
- ⊕ Identify and define the poem's anger by using your best descriptive powers—comparisons, actions, sensory manifestations.
- ⊕ Write with restraint. Rants are pedantic.
- ⊕ Be artful. Bring your reader into your story with common cause.
- ⊕ Humor—irony and satire—can make dark moments more engaging.
- ⊕ Avoid summarizing anger with adjectives and abstractions.

Suggestions for Your Writing

- ⊕ Think of a memory when you really lost your temper. Go back to that time and write a poem that leaves you vindicated.
- ⊕ Think of a time when someone lost his or her temper with you. Write a poem about your perspective and resolve it differently.
- ⊕ Think of a social justice issue. Write about the damage it does.

More Examples of Anger in Poems

Epigram from The French by Alexander Pope
Sir, I admit your general rule,
That every poet is a fool:
But you yourself may serve to show it,
That every fool is not a poet.

Run Away by Denise Lajimodiere
The first time I ran away
my father brought me back.

I ran away again, headed
to Red Lake that winter,
damn near died,
was pretty skinny
when I stumbled
into my father's log cabin
in the bush.
      I was ten
years old. He didn't
say a word, put me to bed.

When the Indian agent kicked
down the door, my father
sat there with a shotgun, aimed.

If We Must Die by Claude McKay
If we must die—let it not be like hogs
Hunted and penned in an inglorious spot,
While round us bark the mad and hungry dogs,
Making their mock at our accursed lot.
If we must die—oh, let us nobly die,
So that our precious blood may not be shed
In vain; then even the monsters we defy
Shall be constrained to honor us though dead!
Oh, Kinsmen! We must meet the common foe;
Though far outnumbered, let us show us brave,
And for their thousand blows deal one deathblow!
What though before us lies the open grave?
Like men we'll face the murderous, cowardly pack,
Pressed to the wall, dying, but fighting back!

Barnes, Barry. We *Sleep in a Burning House*. Mammoth, 2008. 14.
Heffernan, Michael. *Walking Distance: Poems*. Lost Horse Press, 2013. 17.
Lajimodiere, Denise. *Bitter Tears*. Mammoth, 2016. 32.
Padgett, Ron. *Handbook of Poetic Forms*. Teachers & Writers, 1987.
Wagner, Maryfrances. *Dioramas: Poems*. Mammoth, 2015. 85.

DEPRESSION

Depression, sadness, moodiness—all these are symptoms of depression. Ennui is a familiar companion after industrialization. Before the 20th century, poetry is more often about intense emotions, not drudgery of the daily grind. Battles have heroes who engage in hand-to-hand combat, like Achilles and Hector in the *Iliad*. They rage, fight, and die, or live. Love matches are dramatic tragedies like *Romeo and Juliet*. The lament for Barbara Allen celebrates an extraordinary passion. The literary tradition does not include ballads about bored cubicle dwellers. Nor are their poems from enslaved peoples of present or past.

Depression responds to pressures from dehumanization of industrialization.

Ennui and the Industrial Age

Bureaucracy is an enemy with no head nor heart. Unsung heroism comes in anonymous conflicts of modernity, perhaps framed by robocalls. The Absurd Theater hero finds a moral clarity with no hope of reward. Henry David Thoreau states this dilemma well:

> The mass of men lead lives of quiet desperation. What is called resignation is confirmed desperation. From the desperate city you go into the desperate country, and have to console yourself with the bravery of minks and muskrats. (*Essays on Civil Disobedience*)

For Thoreau, nature is still an antidote to civilization's ills, but it exaggerates the alienation of people from natural cycles. The regimentation and mechanization of daily life—heck, just the traffic—create a low-level, dull pain.

In 19th century Ireland, the Great Hunger created a large-scale disaster—a million Irish died, and another million emigrated. The DNA of immigrant descendants shows an "epigenetic" propensity toward depression (Oonagh Walsh in *Stalking Irish Madness*).

In England in the same century, William Wordsworth, Thomas Hardy ("The Ruined Maid"), and William Blake began to publish commentary on the human toll of industrialized societies. These are serious, critical works, sometimes ironic like Blake's poem about child slavery:

The Chimney Sweeper by William Blake
When my mother died I was very young,
And my father sold me while yet my tongue
Could scarcely cry 'weep! 'weep! 'weep! 'weep!
So your chimneys I sweep & in soot I sleep.

There's little Tom Dacre, who cried when his head
That curled like a lamb's back, was shaved, so I said,
"Hush, Tom! never mind it, for when your head's bare,
You know that the soot cannot spoil your white hair."

And so he was quiet, & that very night,
As Tom was a-sleeping he had such a sight!
That thousands of sweepers, Dick, Joe, Ned, & Jack,
Were all of them locked up in coffins of black;

And by came an Angel who had a bright key,
And he opened the coffins & set them all free;
Then down a green plain, leaping, laughing they run,
And wash in a river and shine in the Sun.

Then naked & white, all their bags left behind,
They rise upon clouds, and sport in the wind.
And the Angel told Tom, if he'd be a good boy,
He'd have God for his father & never want joy.

And so Tom awoke; and we rose in the dark
And got with our bags & our brushes to work.
Though the morning was cold, Tom was happy & warm;
So if all do their duty, they need not fear harm.

The undersized boy can fit into chimneys at present, but one day, forced into a chimney, he will suffocate to death. In the poem, the child yearns for a Christian heaven, which is a counterpart to his daily, dangerous toil for Christian households.

    The Industrial Age brought inventions that had potential to improve people's lives. Instead, fragmentation occurred. During World War I, mechanical innovations in weaponry resulted in tremendous slaughter. This created new horror. Religions did not provide easy answers. William Butler Yeats wrote one of the century's most important poems 1919:

The Second Coming, by William Butler Yeats
Turning and turning in the widening gyre
The falcon cannot hear the falconer;
Things fall apart; the centre cannot hold;
Mere anarchy is loosed upon the world,
The blood-dimmed tide is loosed, and everywhere
The ceremony of innocence is drowned;
The best lack all conviction, while the worst
Are full of passionate intensity.

Surely some revelation is at hand;
Surely the Second Coming is at hand.
The Second Coming! Hardly are those words out
When a vast image out of *Spiritus Mundi*
Troubles my sight: somewhere in sands of the desert
A shape with lion body and the head of a man,
A gaze blank and pitiless as the sun,
Is moving its slow thighs, while all about it
Reel shadows of the indignant desert birds.
The darkness drops again; but now I know
That twenty centuries of stony sleep
Were vexed to nightmare by a rocking cradle,
And what rough beast, its hour come round at last,
Slouches towards Bethlehem to be born?

The poetic strategy is to identify, name, give historic context, and prophesize—in the Old Testament sense of the word. Vivid images and allusions to Christianity expand the impact of the poem. It might move the reader to shift from an inactive depressive state to one of action. Sharing awareness is the strategy.

    A contemporary response to mechanization of daily life comes from Donald Levering, who reduces his personal life to car parts:

Waiting for the Repo Man, by Donald Levering
to relieve me of my wheels

impatient for the insurance lady
to deny my claim to the open road

Expecting the divorce court
to cleave my carburetor

and divide my heart
Ready for my drive train
to come unhitched
for my water pump to give

Lining up for the recall
of my ignition

Resigned to futile intention
Anticipating the heat

from the tiny smelters
of my final consumers.

The extended metaphor of man and machine creates an irony, and a novelty, that helps readers to continue to the end. It seems less grim than Yeats's poem. The poem also resembles the blues, considered below, and also has a gallows humor. One of Levering's books is entitled *Car Pool*, about the commuter's life, which the poet renders equally futile.

Oppression and Poetry

Social injustice is another cause for depression. Greek and Roman slaves did not write poetry, so their stories are lost. Little remains of ordinary people's lives through history, especially the oppressed populations. The 19th century in the United States is a time when former slaves like Frederick Douglass and Harriet Jacobs published their autobiographies. Paul Laurence Dunbar (1872-1906) is one of the first poets in the African American poetics of resistance. His parents were slaves; their experience shaped his life as he expresses in this protest:

We Wear the Mask, by Paul Laurence Dunbar
We wear the mask that grins and lies,
It hides our cheeks and shades our eyes, —
This debt we pay to human guile;
With torn and bleeding hearts we smile
And mouth with myriad subtleties,

Why should the world be over-wise,
In counting all our tears and sighs?
Nay, let them only see us, while

> We wear the mask.
> We smile, but oh great Christ, our cries
> To thee from tortured souls arise.
> We sing, but oh the clay is vile
> Beneath our feet, and long the mile,
> But let the world dream otherwise,
> We wear the mask!

This poem implies the daily injustices of enduring "long the mile" as the narrator assumes a "mask that grins and lies." This poem uses description, image, repetition, and rhyme, to create a hymn-like pattern.

Dunbar inspired many other poets, including Langston Hughes, Gwendolyn Brooks, Rita Dove, and Amiri Baraka (Leroi Jones). Claudia Rankine's book *Citizen: An American Lyric* (2014) is in this lineage. Rankine writes a tragic drama of racism set in banal situations, like a conversation she had with a hiring committee member while driving to the airport. The tone is stark.

Dennis Etzel expresses the dehumanization of working in a repetitive food industry job. His book *Fast Food Sonnets* includes short, pithy lyrics about the experience of working at low-paying food industry jobs from 1988 to 1993. Here is a sample from this book:

Cleaning the Flat Grill by Dennis Etzel Jr.

I scrape the carbon off of the flat grill,
as another member from the kitchen
is off—let go—after the manager
yells at him, tells him to mop the back room
before leaving. The grill scraper is sharp—
takes off brown ashes. The manager
jokes with me about something, as a way
to let the boy know he is not wanted.

I push down hard to get the residue
off the metal, wishing for smooth silver
again. The manager turns his back on
the young man he laughs at. I do my best
to nod, smile, continue to scrape away
any hope for this surface to be clean.

Etzel writes in an afterward, "I do not want to make this collection political, but can't help but think of the work we still need to do." He notes the problems of workers' rights and the hierarchy of power. The scraping in this poem is literal as well as figurative.

The Blues

Another response to depression is self-deprecation and exaggeration like the musical blues idiom. It is about failed love (most often), or financial problems (on occasion), or fate itself, like "Born Under a Bad Sign" by Booker T. Jones and William Bell. Its refrain is "I been down since I begin to crawl / If it wasn't for bad luck, / I wouldn't have no luck at all." The narrator puts him or herself into a one-down position, seeking sympathy.

The blues are more intense, and even, oddly, more joyful as repetitions create a transformative spell. Repetition gives singers a chance to bend notes; increase volume or lower it to pianissimo; or shift rhythm. Harmonica, guitar, and voice can mimic weeping, and so create an intertextual commentary. Many blues tunes are about lost loves, sometimes in graphic terms. "Backwater Blues" is a tamer song, about a floodwater victim, recorded by Bessie Smith. It typifies the pitiable condition that the narrator elevates to biblical dimensions.

The Backwater Blues, traditional
It rained five days and the sky turned black as night
It rained five days and the sky turned black as night
There's some trouble taking place in the lowlands at night

I woke up this morning, couldn't even get out of my door
Woke up this morning, couldn't even get out of my door
Sometime there's so much trouble, a girl don't know where to go

They rowed a little boat about five miles across the farm
They rowed a little boat about five miles across the farm
I packed up all my clothes and they rowed me right along

It thunders and lightnings and the wind begins to blow
It thunders and lightnings and the wind begins to blow
There's a thousand people there, ain't got nowhere to go

I went up and stood on a high and lonesome hill
I went up and stood on a high and lonesome hill

I looked down below me on the house I used to live
That's how the blues done caused me to pack up my things and go
Blues done caused me to pack up my things and go
My poor house is gone, I can't live there no more
My poor house is gone, I can't live there no more
My poor house is gone, I can't live there no more

This verse is worth reviewing after the intense hurricane seasons of recent years.

Strategies

Poet do not pretend to cure depression. Some poems are not protest poems, because they do not directly call for action. They may support a social justice cause, but they are more about personal effects of a mechanized daily life, social injustice and oppression, and just plain fate. Their strategies include:

- ⊕ Metaphors or other ways to articulate impersonal forces, like Yeats's "centre that cannot hold."
- ⊕ Use of shorter traditional forms like children's rhymes, hymns, ballads, the blues
- ⊕ Irony—contrast between what should be and what actually exists
- ⊕ Vivid descriptions
- ⊕ Repetitions for emphasis
- ⊕ Play on audience sympathies through examples and shared experience

Suggestions for Your Writing:

- ⊕ Find a favorite short song. Then rewrite it using a political or social cause. Keep the rhythm.
- ⊕ Choose a quotation by a political or social commentator. Expand it to a full-length poem.
- ⊕ Think of an injustice you want to right. Address a poem to an audience that would be sympathetic. Write another to an audience that would not be sympathetic.
- ⊕ Natural disasters—floods, forest fires, tornados, lightning strikes, volcanic eruptions, earthquakes—can inspire a depression poem. Write one that focuses on one part of the experience or the full arc.

More Poems of Depression

Anxiety by D. H. Lawrence
The hoar-frost crumbles in the sun,
  The crisping steam of a train
Melts in the air, while two black birds
  Sweep past the window again.
Along the vacant road, a red
  Bicycle approaches; I wait
In a thaw of anxiety, for the boy
  To leap down at our gate.
He has passed us by; but is it
  Relief that starts in my breast?
Or a deeper bruise of knowing that still
  She has no rest.

**I Wake and Feel the Fell of Dark, Not Day
  by Gerard Manley Hopkins**
I wake and feel the fell of dark, not day.
What hours, O what black hours we have spent
This night! what sights you, heart, saw; ways you went!
And more must, in yet longer light's delay.

With witness I speak this. But where I say
Hours I mean years, mean life. And my lament
Is cries countless, cries like dead letters sent
To dearest him that lives alas! away.

I am gall, I am heartburn. God's most deep decree
Bitter would have me taste: my taste was me;
Bones built in me, flesh filled, blood brimmed the curse.

Selfyeast of spirit a dull dough sours. I see
The lost are like this, and their scourge to be
As I am mine, their sweating selves, but worse.

Etzel, Dennis. *Fast Food Sonnets*. Coal City Press, 2016. 18, 60.
Levering, Donald. "Waiting for the Repo Man." *South 85 Journal*. 2015.
Thoreau, Henry David. *Civil Disobedience and Other Essays.* Dover, 1993.

HUMOR

Humor is one of the most complicated moods. It has two essentials: community and cognitive discord. People share ideas social rules and agreements about natural laws. Humor comes from recognition of the discrepancy between an expected sequential effect and any deviance. A pratfall breaks the walker's gait. A pie in the face breaks social rules.

Poetry has the added trick of certain rhyme and stress patterns that are immediately funny, like limericks. Literary humor also includes: nursery rhymes; incongruity and irony; hyperbole (exaggeration); self-deprecation; ridicule; satire.

A caution: humor works especially well in performances. A former state poet laureate who sells a lot of books told me he only has a few humorous poems, but these are the ones he always reads. He is guaranteed sales when he reads funny poems. Sherman Alexie is well-known for his biting humor at readings, as well as on the written page. He started as a stand-up comedian and developed a literary career later. The influence is noticeable. Performative success is wonderful; happy feedback from a crowd is intoxicating. Poetry has room for humor, but the genre, more importantly, has the capacity to move people in deeper ways. To reduce the poetry palette to humor reduces its power.

Most jokes are one-liners that are great the first time. After the third reading, fourth, fifth—they fall flat. The surprise is over. Shakespeare's sonnet 26, "Shall I compare thee to a summer's day," inspires readers year after year. "Candy is dandy / but liquor is quicker" does not inspire deep thought. Ted Kooser has a wonderful insight into the reduction of poetry to anecdotes, which is like humor:

> Simply to take an anecdote of how you helped your mother wash the car and to cut it up in lines and put it on a page is not enough for anybody. ... The only place that an anecdote is legitimate is as a poem today, and as a result we have tens of thousands of poems that are merely anecdotes.

Kooser's discussion of anecdotes sticks with me, perhaps from a sense of guilt since I have written my fair share of mediocre anecdote poems. Kooser's advice is an important caution for humorists, especially.

Limericks and Nursery Rhymes

The moment an audience hears the beat of the cinquain limerick and hears the aabba rhyme scheme, the context suggests humor, sometimes bawdy and sometimes not. This Edward Lear poem is more of a nursery rhyme:

Limerick aby Edward Lear
There was an Old Man with a beard,
Who said, 'It is just as I feared!
Two Owls and a Hen,
Four Larks and a Wren,
Have all built their nests in my beard!

Children's author A.A. Milne uses a simple rhyme in this well-known poem, and it signals "nursery rhyme" immediately, because of the one-syllable words for a beginning reader and the rhymes:

Now We Are Six by A.A. Milne
When I was one,
I had just begun.
When I was two,
I was nearly new.
When I was three,
I was hardly me.
When I was four,
I was not much more.
When I was five,
I was just alive.
But now I am six,
I'm as clever as clever.
So I think I'll be six
now and forever.

The ironic discrepancy that creates a deeper humor is how the audience knows what the child does not: he is subject to the physical law of sequential time. The delightful rhymes keep interest from one to six. The brevity is just right—one to twenty-one would become tedious.
Former Kansas Poet Laureate Eric McHenry uses this tradition effectively to write about his children:

From Mommy Daddy Evan Sage by Eric McHenry
"Rats!" said Sage, whose magic marker
refused to color any darker.
"Uh-oh. I think I hear them comin',"
I said. "Be careful what you summon.
Rats are responsive. If you call
too loudly you might get them all.
Are you prepared to deal with that?"
She scratched her head. "I guess not. Rat."

McHenry also uses rhyme for this more sophisticated adult poem. It is a self-deprecating look at his post-college years:

Rebuilding Year by Eric McHenry
After Beloit I went back to the paper
and wrote arts features for eight dollars an hour,
and lived in the Gem Building, on the block between
Topeka High with its Gothic tower
and the disheveled Statehouse with its green
dome of oxidizing copper.

I was sorry that I had no view
of old First National. Something obscured it
from my inset balcony. I heard it
imploding, though, like Kansas Avenue
clearing its throat, and saw the gaudy brown
dust-edifice that went up when it came down.

Friday nights I walked to High's home games
and sat high in the bleachers,
and tried to look like a self-knowing new
student, and tried not to see my teachers,
and picked out players with familiar names
and told them what to do.

Repetitions and end-rhymes, as well as internal rhymes, make this resemble an adult nursery rhyme—one for those awkward post-adolescent years. He is making fun of his younger self from the vantage point of an older adult. The implosion of the building parallels his own imploding life, metaphorically. The older youth is out of place at the high school game. Rhyme adds a subtext of irony here.

Adult Humor

A caution for poets who use humor is this: because rhymes are so strongly associated with children's verse in the English language, the tone of humor bleeds into more serious works. I have had students write about serious topics, like grief, but undercut their work by using a child-like pattern. American English has such a large vocabulary, from diverse languages, that rhyming is difficult, often awkward, and often sabotaged by the tradition of children's verse. Rhyme with care.

Adult humor uses more subtle techniques: juxtaposition, the unexpected, self-deprecation, irony, and satire. Narration and bright vocabulary, along with measured lines, can create a vessel for off-center realities. Caryn Mirriam-Goldberg, former poet laureate of Kansas, uses whimsy in her personification of a hotel, including dialogue. The illogic energizes the poem, and the narrator stays in character throughout the poem.

Self-Portrait as Semi-Luxury Hotel
by Caryn Mirriam-Goldberg
Welcome. Kind of. The plant
is fake but tasteful. I do what I can.
At the moment, for example, 11
vacuum cleaners roar the carpeting.
An old woman asks if the salmon
is fresh or wild. The clouds gnaw
on my northern edges.
Someone sneaks a friend into
a discounted room, and the internet
grants you images of me, older, grander.
My awnings ache. My mattresses arch.
I could use what we all could:
the miracle of new white paint,
the sunlight hitting the floating lint
at just the right angle,
and some company to love me.

William Trowbridge, former Poet Laureate of Missouri, has an entire book of Fool poems, *Ship of Fool*. Some are whimsical, some are self-deprecatory, and all explore the trope of the fool in British and American traditions. This is reminiscent of "My Last Duchess" in its use of dramatic monologue, but turned toward humor, not tragedy. This fool poem satirizes philosophers:

The Consolation of Philosophy by William Trowbridge

Fool goes to visit his English cousin Foole,
an unemployed court jester, hoping to find
his roots. Foole, who's been waiting
since 1573 for the jester market to recover,
can't tell him a thing about the ancestors,
though the both doubt there'd be any duke
or archbishops. Actually there are many,
plus seven kings, three saints, and the man
who invented aerosol cheese-spread. The two
go to a pub and drink till they turn philosophical.
"Is matter uniform or multiform?" asks Foole.
"Hume was right," posits Fool. "Cause and effect
is merely a perception." As each pint grows
a brighter halo, they grasp what all the fuss
over pure rational discourse is about.

Trowbridge also has a priceless book of verse written from the point of view of King Kong, *The Complete Book of Kong*.

Strategies for Writing Humor
- ⊕ Be a trickster—challenge the norms. Humor lies beyond decorum
- ⊕ Consider timing—set up the humorous situation, raise the stakes, then throw the punch line. Watch comedians.
- ⊕ Humor depends on the tension between what readers expect and what happens. Strategize disruption.

Suggestions for Your Writing
- ⊕ Write about yourself as a cartoon character, with appropriate dialogue. Perhaps illustrate it.
- ⊕ Once you discover a humorous niche—a sport, roommates, politics, a genre of music, a character like Trowbridge's Fool—develop it in one extended piece or in a series of shorter poems.
- ⊕ Give voice to a piece of furniture. Tell its life.
- ⊕ Think of a day you had that was so bad you had to laugh. Write about it as an extended narrative.

More Humor in Verse

Parties: A Hymn of Hate by Dorothy Parker
I hate Parties;
They bring out the worst in me.

There is the Novelty Affair,
Given by the woman
Who is awfully clever at that sort of thing.
Everybody must come in fancy dress;
They are always eleven Old-Fashioned Girls,
And fourteen Hawaiian gentlemen
Wearing the native costume
Of last season's tennis clothes, with a wreath around the neck.

The hostess introduces a series of clean, home games:
Each participant is given a fair chance
To guess the number of seeds in a cucumber,
Or thread a needle against time,
Or see how many names of wild flowers he knows.
Ice cream in trick formations,
And punch like Volstead used to make
Buoy up the players after the mental strain.
You have to tell the hostess that it's a riot,
And she says she'll just die if you don't come to her next party—
If only a guarantee went with that!

Then there is the Bridge Festival.
The winner is awarded an arts-and-crafts hearth-brush,
And all the rest get garlands of hothouse raspberries.
You cut for partners
And draw the man who wrote the game.
He won't let bygones be bygones;
After each hand
He starts getting personal about your motives in leading clubs,
And one word frequently leads to another.
At the next table
You have one of those partners
Who says it is nothing but a game, after all.
He trumps your ace

And tries to laugh it off.
And yet they shoot men like Elwell.

There is the Day in the Country;
It seems more like a week.
All the contestants are wedged into automobiles,
And you are allotted the space between two ladies
Who close in on you.
The party gets a nice early start,
Because everybody wants to make a long day of it—
They get their wish.
Everyone contributes a basket of lunch;
Each person has it all figured out
That no one else will think of bringing hard-boiled eggs.

There is intensive picking of dogwood,
And no one is quite sure what poison ivy is like;
They find out the next day.
Things start off with a rush.
Everybody joins in the old songs,
And points out cloud effects,
And puts in a good word for the colour of the grass.

But after the first fifty miles,
Nature doesn't go over so big,
And singing belongs to the lost arts.
There is a slight spurt on the homestretch,
And everyone exclaims over how beautiful the lights of the city look—
I'll say they do.

And there is the informal little Dinner Party;
The lowest form of taking nourishment.
The man on your left draws diagrams with a fork,
Illustrating the way he is going to have a new sun-parlour built on;
And the one on your right
Explains how soon business conditions will better, and why.

When the more material part of the evening is over,
You have your choice of listening to the Harry Lauder records,
Or having the hostess hem you in
And show you the snapshots of the baby they took last summer.

Just before you break away,
You mutter something to the host and hostess
About sometime soon you must have them over—
Over your dead body.

I hate Parties;
They bring out the worst in me.

The Great Figure by William Carlos Williams
Among the rain
and lights
I saw the figure 5
in gold
on a red
firetruck
moving tense
unheeded
to gong clangs
siren howls
and wheels rumbling
through the dark city.

Today by Roger Lathbury
Today I turn seventy-two;
I can read, use a hammer and screw.
Everything's fine
Until 8:30, 9—
And then—do you know what I do?

Kooser, Ted. "Interview." Shelly Clark and Marjorie Saiser, editors, *Road Trip: Conversations with Writers*. Omaha: The Backwater Press, 2006. 29.
Lear, Edward. "There was an Old Man with a Beard." *Poetry Foundation*. Web.
McHenry, Eric. "Rebuilding Year." Waywiser Press, 2006. 15.
-----. "Mommy Daddy Evan Sage." Reprinted, with permission, from "Eric McHenry." *A Map of Kansas Literature.* Washburn University. Web.
Milne, A.A. "Now We Are Six." *Family Friend Poems.* Web.
Mirriam-Goldberg, Caryn. *Landed.* Mammoth Publications, 2006. 50.
Trowbridge, William. *Ship of Fool.* Red Hen Press, 2011. 26.

WHIMSY

The riddle, a genre of whimsy, is embedded in the earliest Anglo-Saxon oral literatures. *Merriam-Webster* defines a riddle as: "A mystifying, misleading, or puzzling question posed as a problem to be solved or guessed often as a game." Beyond puzzles and questions, a riddle is, according to Edward Hirsch, "both an interrogative and an expressive form, possibly the earliest form of oral literature—a formulation of thought, a mode of association, a metaphor." Hirsch asserts that riddles are universal contests of wits, from Oedipus Rex to the present. He describes riddles in Sanskrit texts and the Hebrew Bible. Riddles use *double entendres* and other circumlocutions to suggest a word or phrase. These can be instructive, but more often they are pure whimsy. They delight more than instruct.

Wordplay, from nursery rhymes to bawdy limericks, appeals to people's love of games. A well-wrought riddle is in itself a thing of interest, if not beauty. They are verbal versions of the game "charades" and apt entertainment for a long evening.

In the history of British poetics, riddles begin with a set verse form. Contemporary riddlers appeal to people's love of play. The mood of whimsy does not limit itself to a single form.

Anglo-Saxon Riddles

The two-part line, three beats each side, is a common Anglo-Saxon verse form; rhyme depends on alliteration (beginning of word sounds repeated throughout a line). The *Exeter Book of Riddles*, 1000 years old, contains dozens of riddles, some graphically sexual, some not.

[Bookworm]
Moððe word fræt—   me þæt þuhte
wrætlicu wyrd   þa ic þæt wundor gefrægn ,
þæt se wyrm forswealg   wera gied sumes ,
þeof in þystro,   þrymfæstne cwide

ond þæs strangan staþol .   Stælgiest ne wæs
wihte þy gleawra   þe he þam wordum swealg.

A moth ate songs—wolfed words!
That seemed a weird dish—that a worm
Should swallow, dumb thief in the dark,
The songs of a man, his chants of glory,
Their place of strength. That thief-guest
Was no wiser for having swallowed words.

This riddle argues that storytelling is better than saving knowledge in books. The bookworm, or moth caterpillar, can consume velum manuscripts, yet the oral tradition of songs and chants, when held in memory, are beyond such destruction. The book reader may also be no wiser after chewing up such a "cwide" or cud.

Here is an example of a bawdy riddle, in the same verse form in the original but lost here. It rivals any limerick, even after all these centuries:

Riddle 45, Exeter Book
I have heard of a something-or-other,
growing in its nook, swelling and rising,
pushing up its covering. Upon that boneless thing
a cocky-minded young woman took a grip with her hands;
with her apron a lord's daughter covered the tumescent thing.

Here are a couple Mother Goose riddles that have simple end rhymes, in modern English. They are as old as anyone can remember. Perhaps the couplets echo the Anglo-Saxon two-part line:

A Sieve, Anonymous
A riddle, a riddle, as I suppose,
A hundred eyes and never a nose!

A Star
Higher than a house, higher than a tree.
Oh! whatever can that be?

These are simpler than the Exeter riddles, designed to appeal to children. These train the imagination as well as the ear for rhythms of the English language.

Contemporary Riddles

Emily Dickinson writes some of the first serious riddles in U.S. poetry. The riddle form gives this poem, for example, a tone of irony rather than gloom:

Under the Light Yet Under by Emily Dickinson
Under the Light, yet under,
Under the Grass and the Dirt,
Under the Beetle's Cellar
Under the Clover's Root,

Further than Arm could stretch
Were it Giant long,
Further than Sunshine could
Were the Day Year long,

Over the Light, yet over,
Over the Arc of the Bird –
Over the Comet's chimney –
Over the Cubit's Head,

Further than Guess can gallop
Further than Riddle ride –
Oh for a Disc to the Distance
Between Ourselves and the Dead!

The topic of the poem, the "Dead," is held back until the end. It is indirect. It has repetitive descriptions and parallel lines, alliterative like some Anglo-Saxon verse. The architecture of the poem, then, creates suspense. Dickinson also injects whimsy into the details, like the "Beetle's Cellar." Then the contrast to the last line is more extreme. This is an adult poem that borrows from light verse and subverts it.

I borrow a child's riddle form for this sectioned poem about "eyes." Even though the answer is in each section, the uncovering of unexpected places for eyes is the point of the wordplay:

Eye Riddles, by Denise Low
Laser-dot red eyes among green
euonymus sheaves:

    A vireo darts herkie jerky
    on spliced-video film.
    Looped once, looped twice:
    Tweet. Silence. Tweet. Silence.
+
Peony buds drip sap
    striped billiard balls
    red white green white
    eyes squeezed shut.
+
Lookout chipmunk
    its kohl-lined eyes
    point the way
    past pine's
    bare slash.
Tail taut
    black bead eyes
    look
    out.
+
A cat's vertical eyes
    are tandem gyroscopes
    level just so.
    Its body circles
    unmoved elliptical
    twin stars.
+
Dog eyes are brown honey
    traps.
+
Snake eyes
    slit yellow moonlight
    make two wires
    skewering
    tossed ivory
    cubes.
+
Kelly green poison veins
    feed on plump potato flesh.

    Below nubby eye bumps
    Cuzco-line alien lifeforms glow.

+
What
> my father
> saw that night
> the door jamb
> painted
> Evil Eye
> in invisible ink.

> He tells me
> "The Devil is real."

Gertrude Stein was not a child's poet, but her sense of play is apparent in her writing. She upsets readers' expectations of poetry and of syntax:

from *Tender Buttons* - [Eggs] by Gertrude Stein
Kind height, kind in the right stomach with a little sudden mill.

Cunning shawl, cunning shawl to be steady.

In white in white handkerchiefs with little dots in a white belt all shadows are singular they are singular and procured and relieved.

No that is not the cows shame and a precocious sound, it is a bite.

Cut up alone the paved way which is harm. Harm is old boat and a likely dash.

A modernist writer like Gertrude Stein has a whimsical impulse as she deconstructs syntax in its grammatical order.

A poet, always a child learning language, strives to solve poem-riddles. Riddles are battles of the wits in the Bible. See stories of Daniel, Solomon, and Samson. Hirsch dates Sanskrit riddles to Book 1 of the *Rig-Veda* (1700–1100 BCE). Riddles are among the oldest poetic forms. They adapt from comic to serious themes; they take shape in myriad patterns. Whimsy may be a serious business and play. Lewis Carroll's "Jabberwocky" has delighted readers for generations. It is not that far removed from Stein's experimental series *Tender Buttons*. Contemporary riddles work through contrasts, accumulation of details, and extended metaphor.

Strategies for Writing Whimsy

⊕ Traditional humorous forms, like the limerick or the riddle. These use a paint-by-numbers pattern. Half the poet's work is done.
⊕ Humorous haiku can work well and play off the form.
⊕ Wingdings, emoticons, typography—all these can be media of the whimsist writer.
⊕ Imagined beasts, plants, aliens—all magical and real life forms can find roles in whimsy poems.
⊕ Ordinary objects can be re-purposed into whimsical objects. An example is James Tate's poem, "The List of Famous Hats."

Suggestions for Your Writing:

⊕ Go to your kitchen and choose a utensil. Write a riddle about it.
⊕ Choose a favorite flower or simply shaped hand tool. Write a sectioned poem about it in different settings.
⊕ Think of a monster or superhero or villain. Write a poem that describes him/her. Do not give the name until the last line.

More Whimsy Poems

Jabberwocky by Lewis Carroll

'Twas brillig, and the slithy toves
Did gyre and gimble in the wabe:
All mimsy were the borogoves,
And the mome raths outgrabe.

"Beware the Jabberwock, my son!
The jaws that bite, the claws that catch!
Beware the Jubjub bird, and shun
The frumious Bandersnatch!"
He took his vorpal sword in hand:
Long time the manxome foe he sought,
So rested he by the Tumtum tree,
And stood a while in thought.

And, as in uffish thought he stood,
The Jabberwock, with eyes of flame,
Came whiffling through the tulgey wood,
And burbled as it came!
One two! One two! And through and through
The vorpal blade went snicker-snack!

He left it dead, and with its head
He went galumphing back.
"And hast thou slain the Jabberwock?
Come to my arms, my beamish boy!
Oh frabjous day! Callooh! Callay!"
He chortled in his joy.

'Twas brillig, and the slithy toves
Did gyre and gimble in the wabe:
All mimsy were the borogoves,
And the mome raths outgrabe.

The Horrid Voice of Science by Vachel Lindsay
There's machinery in the butterfly;
There's a mainspring to the bee;
There's hydraulics to a daisy,
And contraptions to a tree.

If we could see the birdie
That makes the chirping sound
With x-ray, scientific eyes,
 We could see the wheels go round."

And I hope all men
Who think like this
Will soon lie
Underground.

Some Things That Fly There Be by Emily Dickinson
Some things that fly there be –
Birds—Hours—the Bumblebee --
Of these no Elegy.
Some things that stay there be –
Grief—Hills—Eternity –
Nor this behooveth me.
There are that resting, rise.
Can I expound the skies?
How still the Riddle lies!

The Dark Sofa by Erika Zeitz
Stormy afternoon slams the day shut.
I am caught in its hinges.

Now there is a pulse of pain,
a lion clawing at my skull.

The middle of the house,
so bright. I come home below

to ground level, earth and mold
under the half-finished floor.

I seek the darkest, softest place
to put my feet up.
The old sofa is too narrow to share.
Eyes closed, arms folded

mummy-tight, I lie still,
hope for nothing,

not even a dream.
Rest deeper than the grave.

"The Exeter Book of Riddles"-*Flowers of History*: Incidental Notes after Histories of Roger of Wendover and Matthew Paris. *Univ. of Chicago.edu*
Hirsch, Edward. "Riddle." *Academy of American Poetry.org.*
Low, Denise. *A Casino Bestiary.* Spartan Press, 2017. 13-5.
Robinson, Fred C. "Artful Ambiguities in the Old English 'Book-Moth' Riddle," *Anglo-Saxon Poetry.* Notre Dame Univ. Press, 1975. 355-62.
"Old English Riddles." *Swarthmore College Department of English.* Sept. 2017.

POEMS FOR OCCASIONS

Moods for occasional poems vary, from elegies to celebrations. They focus more specifically on a person or event. The Poetry Foundation defines the occasional poem as: "A poem written to describe or comment on a particular event and often written for a public reading." They give the example of "The Charge of the Light Brigade," written by Alfred, Lord Tennyson for the Crimean War.

Historically, poets are those who cast spells for the ruler, and perhaps this role continues as poets solemnize weddings and publicly console the bereaved. These are occasions when people want to hear speakers proclaim words that unify the wolf pack. I read poetry for my father's funeral and for my son's wedding. As Poet Laureate of Kansas, I once saw my name on the program of the Kansas Arts Commission as the person presenting an "Invocation." I had never seen the word outside of church before then, and it was sobering.

Private occasional poems can be satisfying, because they deepen shared occasions. My grandmother sent a poem every Christmas as an elegant commemoration that family and friends appreciated, even the non-poets. I have done a few, myself. Most occasional poems, however, are for public consumption.

Presidential inaugurations sometimes have poets' invocations. Robert Frost read for John Kennedy's 1961 ceremony, and Bill Clinton asked Maya Angelou to write a poem for his first inaugural address. Angelou wrote the poem, "On the Pulse of Morning." Richard Blanco and Elizabeth Alexander also have had the honor of being inauguration poets.

Occasions can be loopy, like the time the Kansas governor's office asked me, as Poet Laureate, to dedicate the remodeled state legislative chambers. This was a challenge. The result was this extended metaphor comparing a turtle's carapace to the dome of the capitol building:

Kansas Day, January 25, by Denise Low
Long winter nights turtles burrow in mud beds
while we drive icy roads. They rest heavy shells
and sleep. Above them, beavers chink domed lodges
and patrol the waterways. Fishing boats hear their slaps.

And in this season of hard weather we gather,
sheltered by timbers and masonry walls.
We repaint ceilings with star animals and hunters.
We remember "*Ad astra per aspera*" as sun tilts south.

I was asked to write poems to commemorate a Zen master's transmission and the retirement of a Federal Appeals Court Chief Justice.

Wedding poems, epithalamions, are one of the oldest traditions, as these ceremonies are public, spiritual, and celebratory. A Cherokee friend asked me to write a wedding poem, and I drew upon what I have learned from Cherokee elders:

Seven Marriage Offerings, by Denise Low
For Pamela and Michael Tambornino
Ani SaGoNiGe, Offering to the North
Blue skies, clarity, purity of cold wind:
After the winter cleansing we see pines.
Each needle is crisp. This clarity we need.

Ani DaLohNiGe, Offering to the West
The ripe harvest of setting sun, its yellows:
Each evening as we reflect, in tandem,
we share the day's stories and rest.

Ani GvNaGe, Offering to the South
Southern sun heat is passion,
some days too impetuous. In black night,
and in all conflict, we learn compassion.

Ani WoDiGe, Offering to the East
Each morning, without gall, we see sunrise:
Each dawn we are newlyweds, humbled
by the brown river and its red mists.

GaLvLaDi, Offering to the World Above
The heavens rise beyond our sight,
past the sun, moon, planets and stars:
We accept a power beyond our senses.

ELaDi, Offering to the World Below
Beneath us lie the remains of all beings
and the kingdom of rocks and finally
the fire of this planet's hearth: our home.

Offering to the Spirit Within
Heartbeat repeated within us and again,
our own fires, winds, stony bones, muddy flesh:
Two hearts measure out one life

Food festivals, meals, holidays—all these are times when ritual words are appropriate. William Stafford's ode to garlic is a classic. Annie Finch gives a strong endorsement to occasional poems in a short essay, which contains these advantages of the genre:

> Occasional poetry provides me with the opportunity to address a wider audience. I am gratified when someone, perhaps especially someone who doesn't often read poetry, is moved by what I've written. I enjoy the aesthetic challenge of using the traditional tools of the public poem—meter, rhyme, and accessible language—while maintaining a contemporary consciousness and literary standards. I am often genuinely inspired by the very occasionalness of occasions.

Her insights give some guidelines regarding the composition of occasional poems: consider the audience; take on the challenge; stay contemporary; and get inspired.

Some Strategies

Occasional poems are like toasts. They need to refer to the moment and the tradition. They also need to be original. Here are a few suggestions:
- Clearly state the occasion in the title or subtitle and name the relevant names, if necessary. The epigraph is key to date, place, and time.
- Use a regular pattern to signal to the audience that this is a ritual occasion. Parallelism is effective.
- Describe a setting that will ground the occasion.
- Use some universal images that connect to the occasion
- Individualize the poem with reference to the occasion and person or people involved.
- Use humor carefully. This poem needs to add decorum rather than trivialize the moment.

Suggestions for Your Writing

- ⊕ Compose your own elegy. Then compose a poem for your own christening. What differences and similarities do you notice?
- ⊕ Take the day's news events. Choose one about complete strangers and write an occasional poem commemorating it. What essence of the occasional poem form can carry it? What does it lack in personal touches?
- ⊕ Commemorate a book launch for a friend or a similar occasion. After revision, publish it on social media.

More Poems of Occasions

Día de Muertos by Xánath Caraza
The journey begins
Mictlán awaits
The smoke of copal traces the way
And continues to his house

The house of paintings
The house of red windows
Of seasnails
That resounds with the waves

Path of butterflies
Seafoam forging ahead
What is left?
But continue the way

What is left?
But sing the ancestral chants

Lights guide
In the deepest darkness
From afar shining in the red eternity
Leading the souls

Flavors will only be
Reborn tonight

Yellow shadows celebrate
With the scent of *cempaxochitl*
Carved into the sea of blue memory
Into the mirrors of the soul

The heart celebrates with the aroma of copal
Sacred smoke renews of life

The journey begins
Mictlan awaits

Path of yellow shadows
Ascending butterflies
We sing the ancestral chants
Let the seasnails sound
Only tonight
Let the doors open

Let the souls arrive
I am not the same
Mictlan awaits

Chinese New Year by Caleb Puckett

    Thrust behind the red barricade, we observe how the radio tower slits the Great Bear's throat like a razor against silk, while the wind pushes incense from the censer, obscuring the confetti caught on the dragon costumes weaving through those old streets now ground to a fine, white powder by the press and twist of innumerable human pestles marching onward with the convulsions of a fever.

    "It's an anodyne against an archaic horizon armed with stones," said the brochure introducing the New Year to those spectators who must rise with the smoke of celebration.

    "It's an armistice of sorts for those who fear loneliness more than deceit," it continued, ensuring there would be no hesitation once the fireworks landed close enough to suggest the square had turned aggressive, apropos of any fine-minded entertainment scheduled for the denizens posing as object lessons.

General Assembly Poem by Kevin Rabas
Emporia State University (8-18-17)
Walk on campus,
   and you are welcomed
by the hum of mower
   or leaf-blower,
like a drumroll, ushering
you in—to the grass, trimmed,
   the sidewalks swept clean—
everything shiny, new,
   (perhaps) like you.

When you run your finger along
   the page, trace words, parse
what's said—and the heart and intellect
   beneath and in between—you learn
something so many many
   never see: "Knowledge,"
my son says. "Knowledge."

When the spot light moves
   and stops on you, and your
line comes out
   like in conversation
only louder, brighter, and you convince
   and move
the people seated in darkness,
   you know
you've done well,
   you're someone else.

Under the magnifying loop,
   that glass pool,
your hands and a sharp tool
   as you etch
into metal
   a curve, a filigree, a face,
a mirror to the world
   writ small, so so small.
The Bunsen burner flame, thin
   and wavy, flickers to your breath,
moves as you do, as you study

  the lab paper, the instructions
on how to mix and meld
  the blue powder in the spoon.

When you stand
  under the hoop
and jump and jump,
  lofting, tipping
the ball in, orange
  and round and big, like a fruit
into an apple basket,
knowing this is one thing
you can do, when the court
  is bright with light,
make this simple, vital move.

When you reach
  with all your might
and dive, the football
  into your fingers, your hands,
then your chest, knowing
that is as far as you can go,
the limit of your lift, your body,
  your limbs. You leave nothing
on the field, except sweat.

When you splay
  your fingers
on the spongey track
  lunge with all your weight
everything pointed forward.
  You will sprint
into the future, a thick
  white line
on the ground ahead.

And when you pack your things
  for the day back up, put
into your backpack
  your pencils and pens,
your drawing pad, your phone,
  your drumsticks, your lunch:

the orange, the almond nuts—
   and you make the walk
for home, you take something
   else with you, a series
of thoughts and moves, lessons,
like a short movie strip, full
of color and action and sound, but more
   like the memory the tightrope walker has
of treading careful, heel to toe
   over the city, over the canyon,
over the river, over the rocks—
   you remember where you were,
 more than where you are, and every
   old view is now new.

To Sylvia, To Wed by Robert Herrick
Let us, though late, at last, my Silvia, wed;
And loving lie in one devoted bed.
Thy watch may stand, my minutes fly post haste;
No sound calls back the year that once is past.
Then, sweetest Silvia, let's no longer stay;
True love, we know, precipitates delay.
Away with doubts, all scruples hence remove!
No man, at one time, can be wise, and love.

Caraza, Xánath. "Día de Muertos." *Conjuro.* Mammoth, 2012. 61.
Finch, Annie. "Occasioning Poet." *Poetry Foundation Harriet Blog.* Apr. 2009.
Low, Denise. "Seven Marriage Offerings" and "Kansas Day, Jan. 25." *Ghost Stories of the New West.* Woodley Memorial Press, 2010. 37, 95.
"Occasional Poems." Academy of American Poets. *Poets.org.*
Puckett, Caleb. "Chinese New Year." *Fate Lines/Desire Lines.* Mammoth, 2014. 61.

Permissions

Danny Caine, *Uncle Harold's Maxwell House Haggadah,* Etchings Press, 2017.
Harley Elliott, *Darkness at Each Elbow.* Hanging Loose, 1993.
Dennis Etzel, "Cleaning the Flat Grill," *Fast Food Sonnets,* Coal City Pr., 2016.
Joseph Harrington, *Things Come On: [An Amneoir]*, Wesleyan Univ. Pr., 2011.
Michael Heffernan, "Puttanesca," *Walking Distance: Poems.* Lost Horse Press, 2013; and *Margie: The American Journal of Poetry* 1 (2002).
Roger Lathbury, "Today," *FaceBook* 9 Sept. 2017, author's permission.
Donald Levering "Waiting for the Repo Man," *South 85 Journal,* 2015.
Stanley Lombardo and Hackett Publishing Company, translation of Fragments 1 and 71, *Complete Poems and Fragments,* 2017.
Mercedes Lucero, "Defining Things." *In the Garden of Broken Things.* Flutter Press, 2016.
Jo McDougall, "Telling Time," *In the Home of the Famous Dead: Collected Poems.* University of Arkansas Press, 2015.
Eric McHenry, "'Rats!' Said Sage," *Mommy Daddy Evan Sage,* Waywiser Press, 2011; and "Rebuilding Year," *Potscrubber Lullabies,* Waywiser Press, 2006.
Kevin Rabas, "General Assembly," permission of the author.
Linda Rodriguez, "How to Be Alone in Love," *Heart's Migration: Poems.* Tia Chucha Press, 2009.
William Stafford, "Ode to Garlic" from *Ask Me: 100 Essential Poems.* Copyright 1987, 2014 by William Stafford and the Estate of William Stafford. Reprinted with the permission of The Permissions Company, Inc., on behalf of Graywolf Press, www.graywolfpress.org.
William Trowbridge, "Consolation of Philosophy," *Ship of Fool,* Red Hen, 2011.
Erika Zeitz, "The Dark Sofa," permission of the author.

Mammoth Publications authors permissions:
Barry Barnes, "Taker of Limbs," *We Sleep in a Burning House,* 2010.
Xánath Caraza, "Yanga" and "Día De Muertos," *Conjuro,* 2012.
Greg Field, "The Story I Tell You," "Holding My Breath," *Black Heart,* 2014.
Diane Glancy, "Petrified Forest National Park," "Snowman w/Overlay," *It Was Then,* 2012.
DaMaris Hill, "night watch," *Vi-ze-bel*\ *Teks-chers*\, Mammoth, 2015.
Denise Lajimodiere, "Run Away," *Bitter Tears.* Mammoth, 2016.
Stephen Meats, "Fierce Heart," *Dark Dove Descending,* 2013.
Jonathan Holden, "Hunting for Morels," *Glamour,* 2011.
Caryn Mirriam-Goldberg, "Self-Portrait as Semi-Luxury Hotel," *Landed,* 2006.
Caleb Puckett, "Excursion," "Chinese New Year," *Fate Lines/Desire Lines,* 2014.
William Sheldon, "Boards," *Rain Comes Riding,* 2013.
E. Donald Two-Rivers, "Ode," *Fat Cats, Powwows, Other Indian Tales,* 2004.
Maryfrances Wagner, "Black Snakes," *Dioramas,* 2015.

www.ingramcontent.com/pod-product-compliance
Lightning Source LLC
Chambersburg PA
CBHW021015090426
42738CB00007B/790